THE MAD SCIENTIST
HALL OF FAME

THE MAD SCIENTIST HALL OF FAME

Muwahahahaha!

DANIEL H. WILSON and **ANNA C. LONG**
Illustrated by Daniel Heard

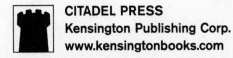

CITADEL PRESS
Kensington Publishing Corp.
www.kensingtonbooks.com

CITADEL PRESS BOOKS are published by

Kensington Publishing Corp.
850 Third Avenue
New York, NY 10022

All Kensington titles, imprints, and distributed lines are available at special quantity
discounts for bulk purchases for sales promotions, premiums, fund-raising,
educational, or institutional use. Special book excerpts or customized printings can
also be created to fit specific needs. For details, write or phone the office of the
Kensington special sales manager: Kensington Publishing Corp.,
850 Third Avenue, New York, NY 10022, attn: Special Sales Department;
phone 1-800-221-2647.

CITADEL PRESS and the Citadel logo are Reg. U.S. Pat. & TM Off.

First printing: August 2008

Book design by Anne Ricigliano

10 9 8 7 6 5 4 3 2 1

Printed in the United States of America

Library of Congress Control Number: 2008922842

ISBN-13: 978-0-8065-2879-3
ISBN-10: 0-8065-2879-6

For Hazel Eve Wilson and Addison Edyn Carmody

Contents

Introduction

For millennia, legions of mad scientists have toiled in underground laboratories, trespassed into the territory of gods, and cackled madly about it into the night. Although the origin of the modern mad scientist is buried in classic literature (think Dr. Frankenstein), it pervades pop culture all the way up to the blockbuster movies of today (think Dr. Evil). And thanks to the machinations of real-life mad scientists, we currently enjoy such inventions as electricity, television, and nonkinetic-directed energy weapons. We have a lot to be thankful for—who else has kept our comic book superheroes on the run, our cities of the future afloat, and our robot hordes well serviced? Yet despite all the happiness and terror that mad scientists have given to us, what have we ever given back to them?

You're reading it. This book honors the greatest mentally unstable geniuses of history in true mad science fashion—by using the tenets of forensic psychology to give them mental autopsies. Starting with child development and proceeding through adolescence and higher education, we will deconstruct the how and why of their abominable plans and heartless transgressions against man and nature. Consider it a little tip of the hat to those fascinating men and women with sky-high IQs, shaky morality, and no fear of stepping into the machines they create. And who knows? With luck, during our descent into the psyches of Earth's most feared and revered mad scientists, we just might find a little spark of mad science in ourselves.

The selection criteria for entry into the Mad Scientist Hall of Fame is a simple measurement of genius and madness: inductees were chosen based on their slippery grasp on reality, mind-blowing discoveries, and killer inventions. Style points were awarded for braininess, ruthlessness, and good old insanityness. As a result, the scientists enshrined in this hall of fame offer a refreshing mix of bold sociopathic behavior and a smooth superintelligence that will never let you down. Truly, these are the maddest of the mad.

We're armed with the skull-cracking power of psychology and we're about to embark on a journey into the mind of the mad scientist. On this field trip, we will identify, categorize, and marvel at the peculiar mental maladies suffered by the biggest geniuses and monsters of modern history. This is what happens when you coax mad scientists out of their laboratories and onto the psychologist's couch. Put on your latex gloves, snap on a pair of goggles, and dig out a lab coat that *isn't* covered in blood stains, because we're about to walk the esteemed corridors of . . . *The Mad Scientist Hall of Fame*.

Disclaimer

The psychological interpretations presented in this book are to be considered only *hypotheses*. No psychological assessment measures were administered to any of the mad scientists, real or fictional, included in this book. No direct behavioral observations of psychological symptoms or functioning were made of the mad scientists included here (although many of them have been caught in action on film). No interviews were conducted with any of the mad scientists included in this book, nor have any interviews been conducted with their creators, relatives, or victims.

The diagnoses provided in this book follow criteria outlined in the *Diagnostic and Statistical Manual of Mental Disorder, Fourth Edition Text Revision* (*DSM–IV-TR*), published by the American Psychiatric Association. This manual employs a *multiaxial* approach to diagnosis. The majority of psychological diagnoses are coded on Axis I and include mood disorders, psychotic disorders, and anxiety disorders. Personality disorders, which are thought to be more "permanent" aspects of functioning, are coded on Axis II. Axis III includes physical disorders and medical conditions. Axis IV describes psychosocial and environmental conditions, such as economic hardship or family strife. Finally, Axis V is coded as the global assessment of functioning or GAF—a number ranging from 0 to 100 that indicates overall level of functioning.

Please note that despite generally adhering to *DSM–IV* diagnostic criteria, none of the diagnoses included in this text should be considered to be actual medical or clinical diagnoses. No mad scientists were harmed during the making of this book.

The Mad Scientist Hall of Fame

BENT ON WORLD DOMINATION

A mad scientist never thinks small. Normal people coach soccer teams and worry about the responsibility of being promoted to line shift manager at Denny's. The most ambitious among us may even yearn to become president of the United States. But the mad scientists in this section would never settle for so little; they sought something greater–absolute power. There are plenty of reasons why: With planet-wide authority comes unheard of wealth, respect, and more statues of yourself than you can shake a chisel at. And never forget, the ladies love a man with absolute power over humankind (and vice versa).

This section explores the mind-set of a group of mad scientists who had the tools and the talent to bring the world to its knees. In each of these cases, symptoms of antisocial personality disorder combine with narcissism or stubborn personality traits to create individuals who are very annoying at best and extremely dangerous to others at worst. Whether designing planet-orbiting mega-lasers or spreading misinformation across an entire nation, these mad scientists could not be satisfied until the entire world trembled beneath their gaze.

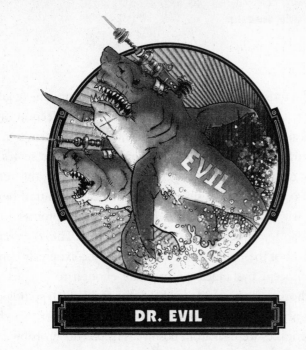

DR. EVIL

(First appeared in the movie *Austin Powers: International Man of Mystery*, 1997)

"I demand the sum of . . . one million dollars!"
—Dr. Evil

Primary goals: Money; world domination
Hair: Bald
Best friend: Miniature clone
Likes: Hot Pockets™
Dislikes: His own son (Scotty)
Hobby: Designing quasi-futuristic clothing
Education: Six years of evil medical school

Genius:

Madness:

Introduction

Perhaps the most coldly frightening and entertaining lunatic genius of all time, the persona of Dr. Evil is an ironic reflection of the stereotypical mad scientist. Like the eccentric Dr. Moreau,[1] Dr. Evil is constantly accompanied by a miniature sidekick who serves as a narcissistic reminder of his own perfection. For Dr. Evil, this version of himself is "Mini Me," a smaller but genetically identical replica, complete with matching suit. Dr. Evil exhibits symptoms of both *antisocial* and *narcissistic personality disorders.* The *comorbidity* (coexistence) of these disorders is rare and can be extremely dangerous for innocent bystanders unfortunate enough to interact with such psychotic individuals. It is likely that Dr. Evil's psychological problems originated in childhood. By his own report, his childhood experiences were far from positive. His parents probably modeled manipulation and violence in their interactions, and the young Dr. Evil likely experienced his parents as cold, uncaring, and punishing. Inherently evil and quite mad, Dr. Evil desires to rule Earth or destroy it—whichever comes first. The only impediment to his plans is a gnarl-toothed, bespectacled secret agent named Austin Powers.

Portrait of a Scientist

Very little is known of Dr. Evil's childhood, but what we do know provides us with startling hints about the origins of the psychological problems that he has experienced as an adult. By his own report, his father was a narcoleptic boulangerie proprietor from Belgium who enjoyed buggery. Dr. Evil reports that his mother, Chloe, was a French prostitute with webbed feet. She was only fif-

---

1. A mad surgeon discussed in another section.

teen years old when Dr. Evil was born. Dr. Evil's father was at least somewhat narcissistic, as he would make outrageously pompous claims, such as his assertion that he was the inventor of the question mark. Dr. Evil's father womanized and drank frequently, would beat Dr. Evil severely, and was by all accounts a very inconsiderate and disagreeable man.

These childhood experiences influenced Dr. Evil in a number of ways. First and foremost, he lacked positive *models* (behavioral examples) of people interacting with one another. Narcissistic parents (such as Dr. Evil's father) are often too self-absorbed to provide unconditional love and affection to their children. This self-centeredness can leave children with no experience of what it is like to be loved and accepted. Without this experience—and especially when punishment is severe—such children will grow up to seek constant attention and approval. They may develop manipulative or unorthodox strategies for getting their needs met, as no typical strategies worked with their parents. Narcissistic parents can also be too self-absorbed to provide appropriate empathetic responses when their children experience pain or hurt, leaving their children no opportunity to learn how to relate to others' feelings. In Dr. Evil's case, he has developed a strong desire for power and control, which he seeks without regard for the impact that his behaviors have on others. This pathological pattern of behavior affects his relationships with his enemies, his employees, and even his own son.

Psychopathology

Dr. Evil exhibits traits of antisocial personality disorder and narcissistic personality disorder, both diagnoses that are typically unlikely to change without intense treatment. His name is apt, as these characteristics are pervasive and observed in long-standing patterns of behavior that have a severe negative influence on his relationships with others (e.g., his homicidal tendencies). He exhibits the following troubling symptoms:

Antisocial irritability and aggressiveness, as indicated by physical fights or assaults. Dr. Evil repeatedly becomes irritable and subsequently assaults his employees. While sitting at his conference table, he enjoys pressing small red buttons that mechanically launch struggling employees from their high-backed conference chairs and into roaring pits of fire. Usually such employees are killed outright, but other times they are only very seriously injured.

Antisocial lack of remorse and empathy. Dr. Evil's maniacal laughter indicates that he enjoys thinking about the suffering of others. He demonstrates no signs of remorse when he sets his employees on fire, and shows positive *affect* (expressed emotion) when he commits assaults on others. In fact, Dr. Evil seems incapable and uninterested in understanding anything from someone else's point of view. He frequently ignores his own son's pleas for attention and understanding, repeatedly telling him to "zip it," or to "shh."

Antisocial illegal activities. Nearly all of Dr. Evil's deeds are illegal, including but not limited to attempting to hold the planet Earth hostage for the sum of 1 million dollars (later amended to 100 billion dollars), assault and attempted murder, "liquidating" the members of his own therapy group, and stealing Austin Powers's mojo. When informed of the economic success of his legitimate companies, Dr. Evil is unimpressed.

Narcissistic grandiose sense of self-importance. Dr. Evil's inflated sense of self-importance is most apparent in his creation of custom-made personal space craft, designed to cryogenically freeze and preserve him for future evil exploits. It is notable that Dr. Evil feels that he is the only person deserving of being frozen and preserved. His sense of self-importance is also belied by the shape of his space craft—one is shaped like a giant "Big Boy" and the other bears a curious resemblance to enormous male genitalia.

Narcissistic preoccupation with fantasies of unlimited success, money, and power. Dr. Evil frequently demands exorbitant sums of money from the United Nations and the president of the United States. While a guest on the *Jerry Springer Show,* Dr. Evil succinctly expressed his desire for power by clutching a globe and declaring, "The world is mine!" to the camera.

Adult Relationships

Dr. Evil's antisocial personality characteristics negatively impact his interactions with nearly everyone. Extremely demanding, he asks his employees to complete ludicrously difficult tasks, such as outfitting sharks with lasers on their heads. Almost every interaction with Austin Powers devolves into either maniacal laughter and a murder attempt, or cowardly fleeing. Clearly, everything Dr. Evil demands in relationships is designed to meet his own selfish needs. Unfortunately, his antisocial tactics for getting his needs met only further distance the very individuals who might provide him with satisfying interpersonal relationships, as these individuals must cope with imminent threats to their lives whenever they interact with Dr. Evil. When Dr. Evil's demands are not met, he becomes childishly pouty and punishes others capriciously.

It should be noted that it is primarily Dr. Evil's narcissistic traits, not his antisocial traits, that interfere in his attempts to build a relationship with his son Scott. Although Dr. Evil is initially willing to accompany Scott to father-son group therapy, he does not seem to take it seriously. When Scott confronts Dr. Evil about his lack of affection as a father, Dr. Evil readily admits to trying to kill him. To make matters worse, Dr. Evil is constantly accompanied by Mini Me, an ill-tempered miniature clone. Dr. Evil is uncharacteristically generous with Mini Me, offering him Hot Pockets and turning a blind eye as Mini Me runs rampant, scrambling onto tables and biting high-ranking employees. Dr. Evil plays charming piano duets with Mini Me but ignores or derides his own son.[2] Dr. Evil even confesses that Mini Me completes him and that he would be inconsolable for at least ten minutes without him. Coming from an empathy-free narcissist, this is love. On the other hand, Dr. Evil dismisses his own son, telling him, "You're the Diet Coke of evil, just one calorie, not evil enough." Ultimately, Dr. Evil sabotages all hope of therapeutic progress with Scott by having the therapy group "liquidated." A last attempt at reconciliation, held during an episode of the *Jerry Springer Show,* ended catastrophically in a full melee, with Jerry Springer biting Dr. Evil's calves.

Scientific Accomplishments

Despite the pervasive negative impact of his psychological problems on his relationships with others, Dr. Evil manages to exploit his evil genius status by surrounding himself with a cadre of brilliant scientists. The scientists who are attracted to the work at Virtucon, Dr. Evil's evil corporation, are motivated by a lust for money and

2. In this memorable scene, Dr. Evil sits at a grand piano and Mini Me perches on the lid of the piano with his own miniature grand piano. This ridiculous and creepy scenario is nearly identical to one found in *The Island of Dr. Moreau,* in which one of Dr. Moreau's genetic mutant children plays a piano duet with him. The miniature piano in that scene is also set atop the larger grand piano.

power. They seem to tolerate Dr. Evil's dangerously whimsical desires because they enjoy creating evil technologies and hope to profit from Dr. Evil's eventual world domination. Together, the research group at Virtucon is a formidable collective of vile minds. Their creative and intellectual genius is evident in a range of advanced contributions in the areas of physics, geology, and biology, including:

- Fully functional time machine
- Subterranean probe designed to explode all of Earth's volcanoes at once
- Moon-based "laser" weapon, dubbed "Death Star"
- Cryogenic freezing pod capable of putting a person into suspended animation
- Slightly finicky command chair with hydraulic lifting capabilities

Additionally, Dr. Evil and his research team have created a moon base and a volcano lair, which demonstrate a superior grasp of both geophysics and space travel. Dr. Evil describes his own evil qualifications best when he tells his son, "You know, Scott, I've been a frickin' evil doctor for thirty frickin' years, okay?"

Conclusion

With such a range of scientific accomplishments, the inhabitants of Earth can count themselves lucky to be alive—only three things stand between Dr. Evil and his goal of world domination. First, although the spy Austin Powers and Dr. Evil have been locked in a battle of wits that spans the twenty-first century, Austin somehow continues to foil Dr. Evil's plans. Second, his own antisocial personality traits lead him to incinerate some of his best scientists, making for high turnover at Virtucon (and occasional lags in production). Finally, his own narcissistic personality traits cause him to frequently execute his cryogenic self-preservation schemes. These schemes keep Dr. Evil intact, but in his absence the people of Earth have time to prepare for his inevitable return.

Diagnosis

Axis I: Parent-child relational problem
Axis II: Antisocial personality disorder; Narcissistic personality disorder
Axis III: No diagnosis
Axis IV: No diagnosis
Axis V: GAF = 55–moderate symptoms: social, occupational challenges; neglects family; frequently defiant to others

TROFIM LYSENKO

(1898–1976)

*"He would have remained a gardener for life,
had it not been for the Soviet regime."*
—Lysenko's father (in a letter to Stalin)

Nationality: Russian
Primary goals: Dominate all of Russian science; avoid learning any science
Hair: Short and slick
Likes: Wheat; eliminating competitors; the USSR
Dislikes: Mendelian genetics; the scientific method
Awards: The Order of Lenin, 1936
Positions: President of the Academy of Agricultural Sciences

Genius:

Madness:

11

Introduction

Trofim Lysenko was a Russian-born layman-scientist who cleverly manipulated the supreme ruler of Russia, Josef Stalin, into believing that he was a scientific genius. Trofim was born a member of the peasant class, but the interference of communism in the scientific establishment gave him the opportunity to cripple a nation's scientific infrastructure. Using his own whimsical version of the scientific method, Trofim fabricated successful experiments and was continuously promoted by political friends. In the meantime, he viciously persecuted competing scientists, sending many to prison camps known as *gulags*. In the process, he set back Russian genetics by more than a century, murdered or imprisoned good scientists, and became one of the most infamous pseudo-scientists of all time.

Portrait of a Scientist

Trofim Lysenko was born in the Ukraine to poor peasant parents. As the oldest of four children, he took on many of the duties of working the family farm and as a result did not learn to read until the age of thirteen. Altogether in his lifetime, Trofim attended about five years of school: two in a village school, two in a horticultural school, and one in a correspondence course for a university degree in agronomy (the study of crops and soil). Not particularly gifted, Trofim was initially rejected to study agriculture at the university after he failed a portion of the entrance exam.[1] Later, he earned his agronomy certificate through a long-distance learning

1. The failed portion of the exam concerned the Scriptures, which could be reflective of Lysenko's morality.

program and began working at a small agricultural research station under the title of "beet selection specialist."

In this position, Trofim was simply a gardener who occasionally educated local farmers about various growing techniques. It was here that Lysenko also learned the fundamentals of grafting species of plants together to from new hybrids. Lysenko remained in the position of glorified gardener until age twenty-seven. He might have remained a beet selector had he not become romantically involved with a married woman and eventually been pressured by her husband to leave town. The beginning of the end of Russian genetics began when young Trofim Lysenko moved to another agricultural station nearby, at Gyandzha.

Scientific Failures, Misinformation, and Showmanship

Lysenko rabidly believed in one massively incorrect idea—the inheritability of acquired characteristics. The *Lamarckian* approach espouses that if a person lifts weights and gains huge biceps (an acquired characteristic) and then has a child, the offspring will be born with more muscle mass (inheritability). While *Mendelian* geneticists around the world had accepted and begun researching the chromosome theory of heredity—the idea that physical characteristics are passed on through genes—Lysenko rejected this theory. Instead, he believed that new strains of plants could be created by exposing the previous generation of plants to environmental influences, such as extreme temperatures. This simplistic idea resonated with the uneducated masses, and Lysenko's own brand of showmanship helped him communicate it well. Lysenko's message, that agricultural production could be massively improved with common-sense innovations, was exactly what people wanted to hear, as opposed to complicated scientific fact. The state of Soviet agriculture was miserable and Lysenko filled a void of hopelessness with his own brand of nonsense.

Lysenko would never have gained public recognition were it not for a single journalist, Vitaly Fyodorovich, who visited the Gyandzha agricultural station where Lysenko worked in 1926. In an article titled "The Winter Fields," Fyodorovich wrote that Lysenko had solved the peasants' problems by planting crops that could grow in the winter, allowing livestock to thrive and fertilizing fields for spring planting. In fact, Lysenko's research focused on getting plants to have a longer growing season; he had only succeeded in growing one patch of peas during a particularly mild winter. Lysenko no doubt knew that the article exaggerated his success at cultivating winter plants, but it also praised him as a "man of the people" who had not studied at a university full of eggheads, but "went straight to the root of things" in his work. Fyodorovich described the agricultural station as a place where Lysenko's pupils and the "luminaries of agronomy visit in the winter, stand before the green fields, and gratefully shake his hand." This first positive publicity whetted Lysenko's appetite for more.[2]

After the article appeared, Trofim changed his research focus to exposing seed to extreme temperatures during germination with the hypothesis that this "vernalization" could toughen the seeds enough to survive growing in the cold Russian winter. This hypothesis was largely unsupported by research, but as time went on political and media forces incessantly supported Lysenko, thanks to the Soviet government's control of media outlets and Lysenko's own natural showmanship. Forming tight relationships with the media and jour-

2. Soyfer, V. (1994), 11. In an ironic foreshadowing, the author of the article described Trofim Lysenko as a serious man, writing that "one recalls only his gloomy eyes, searching the ground with the expression of one contemplating murder, at the very least."

nalists, this mad nonscientist ensured that his ideas were heralded and his experimental results dressed up and lauded. Lysenko and his father tried Lysenko's vernalization process at two sites and harvested a single crop. There were glowing articles about Lysenko's great success, with little proof of the underlying hypothesis.

Lysenko caught the attention of the Communist Party, as he represented the common man's contribution to shared work and the betterment of the collective. At the end of 1929, by a special decree of the Ukrainian Commissariat of Agriculture, Lysenko was given a large laboratory at a major agricultural institute in the Ukraine and gladly left behind his peasant roots and his small research station. Thus, a talented grifter with no university education was put in a position of prominence. It was only the beginning of his lifelong reign of terror.

Psychopathology

Thrust into the big leagues of Russian science, Lysenko quickly exhibited symptoms of antisocial personality disorder, a diagnosis that is all too common in mad scientists bent on world domination. Throughout his career, Lysenko got along well with journalists and politicians but never fit in with legitimate scientists. Several distasteful symptoms of this disorder appeared during Lysenko's career.

Seizes power at all costs. Individuals with antisocial personality disorder may inflict harm on others and show no remorse about it. In a public forum, Lysenko systematically persecuted and eliminated scientists who disagreed with his views, in a manner reminiscent of Dr. Evil.[3] At one agricultural conference, a scientist named

3. Dr. Evil routinely attempts to eliminate anyone with opposing viewpoints, including his coworkers, his own son, and an entire therapy group.

Maksimov critiqued Lysenko's presentation—a common event at a scientific meeting. Lysenko took it personally and later ruined Maksimov by having him arrested for suspicion of subversive political activities.

Success only reinforced Lysenko's sense of power over others. With the powerful help of Stalin and the Communist Party, he rose to membership in the Ukrainian Academy of Sciences in 1934 and president of the Lenin Academy of All Sciences in 1938. Nevertheless, Lysenko rarely published scientific papers. What he did produce reportedly resembled high school laboratory exercises more than advanced research.[4]

Lysenko rarely used previously published equations to interpret his data, presumably because he did not know how to. As he gained power, however, he actually stated that the equations of physics and mathematics were of no use to biologists anyway.

Not afraid to eliminate the competition. Trofim Lysenko pursued his career with murderous intent. Demonized by Lysenko, the head of the national Genetics Institute, Nikolai Vavilov, was fired because of his belief in the (correct) concept that an organism is composed of a mosaic of genes. Worse yet, Vavilov was labeled as a "reactionary" scientist who was acting in a hostile manner toward Soviet academician Lysenko. Vavilov's institute of more than fourteen genetic experts was disbanded, his publications were suppressed, and Vavilov was secretly arrested (the Soviet-controlled press falsely announced that he was studying agricultural conditions in the Carpathian mountains). Vavilov was tortured for two weeks until he confessed to participating in anti-Soviet activities. His compulsory death sentence was reduced to twenty years of imprison-

4. In one 1929 monogram, Lysenko included 110 pages of tables of raw data—something no other scientists did.

ment, where he starved to death. In the meantime, Lysenko glee-fully assumed control of the Genetics Institute.

Participates in serial murder and wanton destruction. Using Vavilov as an example, Lysenko wiped out many "enemy nests" of scientists. Special courts of "honor" were appointed by the Communist government to try those who spoke out against the motherland. Many scientists went to prison for openly defending their views about the inadequacy of Lysenko's work. Others escaped persecution by moving their research to Siberia or by changing careers entirely. Unfortunately, Lysenko's political aspirations and tendency to have his enemies arrested led to Russia's loss of a number of prominent scientists, including

- *Professor Zhebrak*, the president of the Belarusian Academy of Sciences, agreed with a foreign geneticist who critiqued Lysenko's ideas. As a result, Zhebrak was brought to trial and removed as president, but when state police raided his home he had already escaped and hidden with friends.
- *A. K. Koltsov*, who had predicted the double helix structure of DNA twenty years before it was discovered by Watson and Crick, was removed from his university position.
- *Sergei Chetverikov*, the father of population genetics, died in prison while the Western world was lauding his work.

More than ten other scientists died in prisons and gulags and others were shot under mysterious circumstances.

Wields a charismatic personality. Individuals with antisocial personality disorder are often more dangerous when they have charming and charismatic abilities. Lysenko continuously charmed his way out of trouble. By 1948, scientists finally felt safe criticizing

Lysenko's views on heredity, thanks to overwhelming research. Ever the showman, Lysenko dodged criticism by claiming to be working on a "secret project" to develop a variety of branched wheat. In truth, Stalin had received samples of branched wheat from Georgian farms and personally given them to Lysenko. News of this new achievement leaked to the press and Lysenko claimed to be the originator of the idea of branched wheat, though it had been observed and discussed in the agricultural literature for years. This new recognition allowed him to continue his antisocial persecution of Soviet geneticists. Because of Lysenko's unending quest for power and domination, books were burned, articles kept from publication, and a nation previously known as a top research powerhouse went scientifically bankrupt.

Inadequate Scientific Education and Stubbornness

At the apex of his power, Lysenko promoted a number of ideas about agriculture that can be scientifically described as "profoundly stupid." Despite being advanced at charming politicians, his lack of formal education remained obvious in true scientific circles as he engaged in a number of very unscientific behaviors:

Championed ideas without supporting them with evidence. Stalin told the people that he would change the Soviet landscape and massively increase agricultural production. Based on input from Lysenko, the plan included planting strips of forest to block storm winds, digging ponds to encourage wildlife proliferation in forest strips, and completely transforming the natural arid landscape that currently grew wheat, beets, and sunflowers. Lysenko spearheaded the forest planting methods and insisted that all forests were to be planted exactly as he suggested (six or seven acorns in five to six clustered holes). His explanation for this planting method was the need to take advantage of plants' "social activity" of dying when they are the smallest plants in a cluster of the same species. He did not support this idea with any evidence or research. Not surprising, nobody argued.

Worked outside his area of expertise. Although he knew nothing about animal science, Lysenko used his power to advance ridiculous ideas in that field as well. In a public lecture, Lysenko announced with utmost sincerity that it was likely that warblers had given birth to cuckoos by changing their diet to a cuckoo diet. He also spearheaded a revolutionary project that overfed cows in the hopes that their offspring would produce higher fat content milk. Needless to say, this did not work; the offspring produced milk with the amount of fat they were genetically programmed to make.

Refused to admit defeat in the face of overwhelming evidence. Even when vast cluster plantings failed year after year, Lysenko rabidly stuck to his cluster planting plan. Despite achieving no positive results with increasing the fat content of cow milk, Lysenko stubbornly proceeded with these experiments for years.

Conclusion

Ronald A. Fisher, a British geneticist, wrote about how Lysenko was ruining Russian science in 1948. After examining the evidence, he declared that Lysenko was not interested in advancing science or helping poor peasants. Instead, Fisher concluded that the reward Lysenko got out of his work was power: "Power for himself, power to threaten, power to torture, power to kill." This hunger for power was rooted in Lysenko's antisocial personality traits and supported by his stubborn characteristics and charisma all the way until his death of natural causes in 1976 as an old man.

Diagnosis

Axis I: Academic problems; Occupational problems
Axis II: Antisocial personality disorder
Axis III: No diagnosis
Axis IV: No diagnosis
Axis V: GAF = 60—mild symptoms: hurts others; socially effective

5. Fisher, Ronald (1948). "What Sort of Man Is Lysenko?" *Listener*, 40:875.

DR. JULIUS NO

(First appeared in Ian Fleming's novel *Dr. No*, 1958)

"I never fail, Mr. Bond."
—Dr. Julius No

Ethnicity: Chinese and German
Primary goals: Gain ultimate power over humankind; remain laid-back, no matter what
Hair: Slick
Futuristic feature: Bionic metal hands
Likes: Crab Key Island; fine champagne; modern furniture
Dislikes: James Bond; the U.S. and Russian governments
Gang affiliations: The Tongs, a criminal society in China

Genius:

Madness:

21

Introduction

As the arch-villain of the first official James Bond movie, Dr. No is an unforgettable island-bound psychopath with a penchant for torture. Like any villainous supergenius, Dr. No exploits his indigenous workers, imprisons his intruders in order to savor killing them, and operates a completely functioning nuclear reactor in his basement. Unlike most mad scientists, Dr. No exudes a laid-back style and icy calm despite the constant baiting of a very rude James Bond. Such high levels of intelligence and control (not to mention nuclear capabilities) are dangerous weapons in the hands of a scientist who exhibits severe symptoms of antisocial and narcissistic personality disorders. Unsurprisingly, Dr. No was ultimately revealed as an agent for the infamous S.P.E.C.T.R.E. organization.[1] Given that Dr. No was plotting to conquer the world (and quite capable of it), it is fortunate that he met his demise at the hands of Bond—James Bond.

Portrait of a Scientist

Dr. No describes himself as the "unwanted child of a German missionary and a Chinese girl of a good family," and records indicate that Dr. No was born in Peking and raised by an aunt.[2] According to Dr. No, his father was cold and rejecting, to the point that young Dr. No chose to rename himself in a symbolic gesture of hatred toward his father. Dr. No's given name is unknown, but "Julius" was his father's first name. In blatant rejection of his father, Dr. No chose to be called by the last name "No."

Despite these difficult beginnings, Dr. No was a bright child and

1. S.P.E.C.T.R.E. stands for "Special Executive for Counterintelligence, Terrorism, Revenge, and Extortion."
2. This bluntly delivered family tree is eerily similar to that of the notorious Dr. Evil.

managed to maintain educational achievements. He received a good education while growing up in China, despite his involvement with a very powerful criminal organization called the Tong gang. It is unclear where Dr. No learned about atomic energy and nuclear science, but he must have gotten some level of graduate education in these topics. It is known that he attended medical school in Wisconsin for a time and that he began calling himself a doctor after leaving school (although he never graduated).

Scientific and Criminal Achievements

Based on his scientific achievements, Dr. No was primarily trained as a nuclear scientist. However, there is no evidence that he ever worked in the nuclear industry. In Shanghai, Dr. No worked as the treasurer for the Tongs. Rising through the ranks, Dr. No was eventually smuggled into New York City, where he helped run the American branch of the Tong gang. Working for a criminal organization was not enough for the power-hungry Dr. No, and he eventually stole a significant amount of gold bullion from the Tongs.[3] To put it lightly, the Tongs were no longer interested in employing him after this incident.

Dr. No reportedly sought employment with both the U.S. and Russian governments, but was rejected due to his criminal background and thus forced to continue to lead a life of crime. S.P.E.C.T.R.E. is a terrorist organization whose primary mission is to take over the world by causing major world superpowers to fight among themselves.[4] As an affiliate of the S.P.E.C.T.R.E. criminal

3. The amount that Dr. No stole from the Tongs is rumored to be between $1 million and $10 million worth of gold bullion.
4. S.P.E.C.T.R.E.'s scientists likely provided the blueprint of an evil organization for Dr. Evil and his fellow criminals at the misnamed "Virtucon."

organization, Dr. No retreats to a secret island laboratory in Jamaica.[5]

As an island criminal, Dr. No finally begins to show his true scientific and manipulative prowess. Taking a cue from the Tong gang, Dr. No builds up a mining business as a cover for his illegal activities.[6] He recruits half-Chinese workers who are loyal to the point of sacrificing their lives and resides in an amazing modern living space that is built securely into the rock of the island. The entire operation is physically fortified by rock, but

5. Dr. No is not the only mad scientist who has relied on the isolation of an island to maintain a veil of secrecy. Dr. Moreau and Captain Nemo also used uncharted islands as bases of operations.

6. Dr. No hides his activities behind a lucrative guano collection business.

also socially fortified via a variety of lies and manipulations. Dr. No strictly regulates the comings and goings of his workers, and starts a rumor that a dangerous dragon lives on the island, which scares the locals away. Finally, Dr. No keeps himself hidden when speaking to his workers, maintaining a sense of distance and power over them.

The doctor rapidly builds a smoothly operating nuclear reactor on the island, which he uses to fuel his evil plans. Unfortunately, he uses his knowledge of atomic energy to wreak havoc, destroying American rockets from a distance, stealing nuclear weapons, and murdering British secret agents. Dr. No also demonstrates a fair knowledge of poisons.[7] At one point, he paralyzes James Bond with a poison, and when a worker fails to kill James Bond as instructed, Dr. No kills him with a poisonous spider. In addition, workers are provided with cyanide-laced cigarettes so that they can commit suicide before divulging secrets. Predictably, Dr. No uses his scientific knowledge to blow things up and to kill people, rather than working on creative applications of nuclear physics.

Psychopathology: The Roots of Aggression

Like many mad scientists, Dr. No exhibits symptoms of antisocial personality disorder, a pervasive and enduring pattern of disregard for and violation of the rights of others.[8] Aggressive behaviors that indicate reckless disregard for other people's safety are a major feature of this disorder, and Dr. No exhibits aggressive behaviors on a number of occasions. He poisons a fellow scientist, assaults James Bond multiple times during an action-packed fight, and callously orders his workers to physically injure and kill innocent bystanders.

7. Sidney Gottlieb clearly had superior knowledge of poisons.
8. See Dr. Evil (pp. 3–10) for a more complete description of antisocial personality disorder symptoms.

In Dr. No's case, there are a number of factors that likely contributed to his aggressive behaviors.

Parental rejection. There is substantial evidence that Dr. No experienced significant *parental rejection*, the absence or withdrawal of warmth, love, or affection from his parents. He was raised by an aunt and clearly chose his name out of animosity toward his father, Julius. Research indicates that as children enter adolescence, their *perception* of parental rejection leads to increased depression and aggression. Based on his descriptions, Dr. No obviously perceived that his parents rejected him, which likely accelerated his hostile and aggressive behaviors toward others. Additionally, children who experience parental rejection are more likely to have trouble forming close romantic relationships. This may be true for Dr. No, as he does not appear to have established any intimate relationships on his romantically secluded island resort.

Ongoing rejection in adulthood. Dr. No's experience of being rejected continued into his adult life, as he was rejected by a number of employers. When an individual consistently experiences rejection, they are likely to develop a negative view of the social world. This *worldview* is the overarching belief that other people are hostile or threatening. Individuals like Dr. No who hold negative worldviews are more likely to behave aggressively—a preemptive attack on a world that has wronged them too many times.

Exposure to criminality. Dr. No was involved in a criminal organization (the Tongs) from a young age, which likely led him to witness violence on a number of occasions. Involvement with gangs is thought to be partially prompted by a lack of connection with family or school, which was certainly Dr. No's situation. Exposure to violence provides young people with *models* (behavioral examples) for violent and aggressive behavior that then become *mental models* (internalized examples of behavior) and part of their worldview.

Inflated sense of self-worth. Dr. No also demonstrated a number of symptoms of narcissistic personality disorder, which further contributed to his aggressive behaviors. Individuals with this disorder have a pervasive sense of self-importance and grandiosity. In Dr. No, this is seen most clearly in his presentation when he interacts with James Bond. Throughout his conversation, Dr. No presents an extraordinarily flat affect, or emotional display. This behavior seems to stem from an air of narcissistic detachment and superiority. Dr. No also mentions that he believes he is more intelligent than the leaders of all the superpowers, a clearly narcissistic symptom of believing oneself to be very special, unique, and important. To fuel his narcissistic tendencies, Dr. No requires excessive admiration and places a huge value on being treated with respect. When individuals do not properly admire and acknowledge Dr. No's genius, his aggressive tendencies step in to help him exact revenge. Thus, Dr. No's narcissistic tendencies directly contribute to aggressive and antisocial behaviors. Taken together, Dr. No's psychological symptoms make him a dangerous and effective criminal.

Death-Trap Bionic Hands: Dextrocardia or Nuclear Explosion?

In an unusual (and perhaps unavoidable) lapse of style, Dr. No sports a pair of bionic metal hands sheathed in black rubber gloves. These hands provide Dr. No with adequate *gross motor skills,* the coordination between the brain and large muscle groups in our torsos, arms, and legs that allow for such movements as running, jumping, and moving extremities. During an otherwise civil dinner,

Dr. No demonstrates the frighteningly strong crushing power of his hands. Unfortunately, these powerful metal hands make him less accomplished in the area of *fine motor skills*, the coordination between the brain and small muscles, like those in our mouths, hands, and fingers. Fine motor skills allow us to perform such activities as writing, twisting doorknobs, and eating without having things fall out of our mouths. Despite increased strength, it is likely that given the choice Dr. No would rather have his original human hands.

There is conflicting information about the circumstances that led Dr. No to lose his hands. In one version of the story, he loses his hands in a nuclear explosion. In a more complex version, the Tong gang captures and tortures Dr. No in an attempt to find their stolen gold bullion. Dr. No refuses to tell, and the Tongs cut off his hands and shoot him in the chest, leaving him for dead. In a lucky twist of fate, Dr. No survives because he suffers from a rare medical condition known as *dextrocardia* in which his heart is located on his right side. This incident reportedly prompts Dr. No to go to medical school, learn how to fashion prosthetic hands for himself, and transform himself into Dr. No.

Unfortunately for Dr. No, fine motor control is crucial for accomplishing a range of activities of daily living that involve gripping, grasping, and manipulating small objects. Ultimately, Dr. No's poorly designed prosthetic hands lead to his excruciatingly painful death. James Bond and Dr. No fall into the cooling water of Dr. No's nuclear reactor after Bond has caused it to malfunction. Bond is able to escape by grabbing a metal railing and pulling himself out. The physically disabled Dr. No cannot climb out of the water—his hands are just too clunky to grab the railing. As a result, Dr. No boils to death.

Conclusion

Dr. No suffered from poorly designed prosthetics, flat affect, and symptoms of antisocial and narcissistic personality disorders. His knowledge of nuclear physics was advanced, but restricted to relatively mundane evil applications that lacked innovation. The young Dr. No suffered parental rejection that seems to have been compounded later in life by additional rejection, leading him to gang and criminal involvement and aggression toward others. This is unfortunate, as without these crippling psychological disorders Dr. No could easily have used his intelligence and thoughtful demeanor to make significant scientific discoveries or to found profitable non-criminal business interests. Despite his shortcomings, however, Dr. No set the mold for all future brilliant mega-villains—he was an impeccable dresser, an amazing interior decorator, and an ice-cold master manipulator.

Diagnosis

Axis I: Occupational problems

Axis II: Antisocial personality disorder; Narcissistic personality disorder

Axis III: Dextrocardia; Bilateral hand amputation

Axis IV: No diagnosis

Axis V: GAF = 45–serious impairment: murderous tendencies; flat affect; no friends

Intrepid
Explorers of the Great Abyss

The human body may be frail and weak, but the mind of a mad scientist is a great and mighty example of the wonders of nature. By harnessing the power of mental gymnastics, certain mad scientists are able to carve solid mechanical creations from theoretical musings. These inventions—mighty atomic-powered machines or clever protective gadgets—have the power to carry their delicate human masters to the edge of the abyss, and more important, back.

This section tracks down the mad scientists who risked life and limb to peek over the next mountaintop. Unlike stereotypical scientists who lurk in empty laboratories, these adventurers go out into the natural world seeking adventure. Their discoveries are not found in a microscope or telescope, but in the farthest reaches of the natural world—places that were previously off-limits to humankind. Though not necessarily sane, these mad scientists are brave; they are driven to risk their own lives in a quest not for power, but for knowledge.

AUGUSTE PICCARD

(1884–1962)

"[Cigarette smoking is] a dirty habit that should be banned from America by the Government, instead of moderate alcoholic drinking."
—Auguste Piccard (during the Prohibition)

Nationality: Swiss born, Belgian
Primary goals: Journey higher than the highest mountain, deeper than the deepest sea
Neck: Notably thin and lengthy[1]
Hair: A wispy version of the infamous "science mullet"[2]
Headwear: Upside-down basket, worn as a protective helmet

1. The press referred to Auguste as "bird necked." The cartoonist Hergé described his cartoon scientist Cuthbert Calculus as a mini-Piccard, citing the real Piccard's long neck as the obstacle to being able to fully emulate him in a cartoon frame.
2. See Professor Calculus, pp. 42–49.

Stroke of genius: Idea of a pressurized cockpit

Dislikes: Sea level; the press; cigarettes

Twin brother: Jean Felix Piccard, a chemist, balloonist, and aeronautical engineer

Award: Knighted in the Belgian Order of Leopold

Genius:

Madness:

Introduction

Known as the "Admiral of the Abyss," Piccard soared to great heights and dove to great depths, having pioneered the construction of high-altitude balloons and steel-reinforced bathyscapes (known today as submarines). Fans of *Star Trek* will recognize this real scientist and explorer as the namesake of Captain Jean-Luc Piccard, also an intrepid explorer.[3] Like the captain of the *Starship Enterprise*, Auguste was studious but somehow dashing. His scientific adventures earned Piccard sensational attention from the press as he broke altitude and depth records across Europe. A normal scientist under extraordinary scrutiny by the world, Auguste successfully hid his social anxieties beneath his famous and eccentric exterior and rose above petty squabbles.

Portrait of a Scientist

Auguste's family of origin was full of scientists and adventurers. His father, Jules Piccard, was a chemistry professor, and his uncle, Paul

---

3. Jean-Luc Piccard was named after Auguste and his brother Jean Felix.

Piccard, worked in hydroelectrics. Steeped in science from birth, Auguste and his identical twin brother, Jean Felix, both earned doctoral degrees at the Zurich Polytechnical Institute. After taking their first balloon flight in 1913, Auguste and Jean Felix both became balloonists with the Swiss Army's balloon section, a unit dedicated to watching troop movements from the air and directing gunfire. The Piccard family instilled a sense of adventure in Auguste that was to become a fundamental part of his personality.

Like other mad scientists, Auguste engaged in a number of tricky and deceptive capers as a child; however, most mad scientists didn't have an identical twin.[4] It is reported that Auguste once landed a job posing for a sculptor and Jean Felix would sneak in to replace him when he needed a break. The Piccard twins got paid to pose but individually only had to hold still for half the time. The boyish tricks continued as graduate students. Auguste once bet a barber that he had the fastest growing beard the barber had ever seen. Not long after the barber shaved Auguste, he sent in Jean Felix, who was sporting three weeks of facial hair. Auguste and Jean Felix continued to work together to hatch great schemes into adulthood.

Curiosity Prompts Invention, Innovation, and Fame

Piccard's initial purpose in designing a balloon was to collect data about the intensity of cosmic rays in the stratosphere (about ten miles up). He hypothesized that cosmic rays would become more intense the farther the balloon got outside Earth's atmosphere, but there was no existing evidence. It was curiosity about a scientific question—not a need to become a daredevil—that led Piccard to invent a floating machine that could keep a human being alive in the stratosphere. Being unprotected in the stratosphere is no fun:

4. Milgram also engaged in deceptive behaviors with his brother.

First, you bleed from the ears, nose, and mouth, and then you pass out and suffocate. In 1930, Piccard developed the pressurized cabin, which maintains a normal sea-level atmospheric pressure no matter how high the balloon soars.

Like other mad scientists, Auguste was not afraid to test-drive his own inventions. While onlookers were dubious that his pressurized cabin would remain airtight at high altitudes, Auguste did not hesitate to risk his own life. In 1931, he took his balloon for a seventeen-hour flight, hermetically sealing himself and young Charles Kipfer (a research assistant) inside and setting a then world record for altitude (51,775 feet, much higher than airplanes fly today).[5] The flight was risky, but the men wore upside-down wicker baskets lined with pillows to protect their heads. Unfortunately, the flight took hours longer than Auguste had planned due to equipment failure. Rumors spread across Europe that the men were floating in a sky coffin. In fact, Piccard's bright idea to paint the exterior of the gondola black had resulted in 106-degree temperatures inside—despite the chilling 75 degrees below zero in the stratosphere outside. Ultimately, Piccard and Kipfer ran out of water and were forced to make an unexpected late-night landing on a glacier. The adventurers worked through the night on their equipment before they were helped down the mountain by a rescue team.[6]

Auguste's flights led to an amazing amount of media attention. Like Marie Curie, he suffered from the constant buzz of the paparazzi.[7] The press was waiting for him at every landing, hungry for details about his adventures and the hardships he had suffered

5. A year later, Auguste broke his own record with a 53,153-foot flight.
6. Kipfer's parents reportedly forbade him to go on Piccard's next flight.
7. Marie and Auguste also had Einstein in common as a friend and colleague. Marie attended conferences with Einstein, while Auguste consulted with Einstein about how to best record radioactive information in his balloons.

in the skies. Auguste's press attention was generally positive, if slightly mean spirited. The press couldn't get enough of Piccard's captivating character, describing him as excited, bewildered, frail, spindly, bushy haired, wispy, and even bird necked. When Piccard scoffed about another scientist's idea that wind only blew in an easterly direction in the stratosphere, he was quoted. When he gave his nephew a beret, it was heralded as news. In 1933, the press was so interested in Auguste that the People column of *Time* magazine reported it when Piccard cut his "cyclone of hair."[8] Auguste continued setting altitude records, collecting valuable atmospheric data, and having his hair mentioned in the press through the late 1930s.

The years of dangerous high-altitude flights were exhilarating to Piccard, but exhausting for his wife. Finally, he swore to her that he would never take another balloon ride to the stratosphere. Luckily, this became his chance to indulge in a childhood dream. In the same way that Philo Farnsworth had envisioned television while he was still a student, Auguste Piccard had always dreamed of a deep sea–diving vessel that would allow the scientist to navigate independently under water.[9] From a scientific (and safety) perspective, the bathyscape problem was much more difficult than the balloon problem. For most of the 1930s, undersea exploration required that the bathyscape be tethered to a larger ship and only vertical movement had been achieved, as propellers (for horizontal movement) and ballast systems (for up and down movement) had not yet been combined. After spending years researching and testing a variety of combinations, Piccard finally hit on a successful model

8. With the amount of press Piccard received it is no surprise that Hergé based his cartoon professor on him. A 1932 article ("Sentimental Journey," *Time*, April 29) even said that Auguste looked "precisely like a cartoonist's idea of a scientist."

9. Captain Nemo designed a similar submarine craft, although he was motivated less by a desire to explore than by a need to escape from the surface world.

that combined traditional ballast systems and a hull filled with buoyant gas. Another bonus: the undersea gondola did not require Piccard to wear an upside-down, pillow-filled basket for head protection.

Psychopathology: Performance Anxiety

As a scientist thrust into the limelight, Auguste Piccard demonstrated a number of symptoms of *social phobia* also known as *social anxiety disorder*. Social anxiety disorders are relatively common in the general population; up to 13 percent of adults will meet criteria for social anxiety disorder in their lifetime. Anxiety can increase after stressful events and Piccard's travels to the stratosphere certainly may have contributed. Social anxiety disorders are defined by a persistent fear of social or performance situations in which the individual is exposed to unknown people or to possible scrutiny.

Fear of the press. Piccard feared questioning and scrutiny by the press and he directly expressed this fear on a number of occasions. Anticipating a trip to Manhattan prior to a deep sea–diving adventure, Auguste declared that the sharklike reporters in New York were what scared him the most.

Fear of public speaking. On at least one occasion, Piccard showed anxiety related to public speaking. He was giving a speech in Cleveland, when something went wrong with the presentation equipment. When the audience laughed, he reportedly yelled at them to shut up. When the sounds of a musical performance came from the room next door, he reportedly yelled "stop!" until the performance was postponed. These behaviors certainly indicate that Piccard was markedly anxious about his performance, to the point of being nervous, frazzled, and on edge.

Fear of embarrassment. Individuals with social phobias fear that they will do something embarrassing or humiliating. Piccard was certainly aware of other people's opinions about him. When he cut his wild hair short and was asked why he was sporting a new "do," Piccard earnestly told reporters, "Lots of people always laughed at the one that I had before."[10] Statements like these suggest that Auguste may have had excessive levels of fear about people's responses to him and may have been overly aware of what people thought of him and his hair.

Coping with fear. Social anxiety disorders often go undiagnosed because many individuals can either avoid or endure uncomfortable and anxiety-provoking situations. Piccard's fears may have been inconvenient for him at times, but they do not seem to have interfered significantly with his daily life and activities. In fact, Piccard's fear of the press did not keep him from using them to his advantage. For example, in 1937, Piccard sought out the press in order to announce that he needed a corporate sponsor to provide $60,000 for his next balloon. He refused to take money from alcohol or tobacco companies, but was quoted as saying, "Any firm dealing in soap, motorcars, vacuum cleaners or whatnot will do."[11]

Approach Motivation: Auguste the Sensation Seeker

While he may have been anxious to avoid the press, Piccard could not keep himself from the stratosphere. Most modern psychology researchers believe that our adult personalities are based in part on biologically based tendencies to *approach* or *avoid novel stimuli*.

10. "Names Make News," *Time*, October 30, 1933.
11. "Names Make News," *Time*, April 19, 1937.

Novel stimuli are simply any objects or experiences in the environment that are new or unknown. As humans, we have a range of individual differences in approach and avoidance motivations.

These tendencies are easily observed in toddlers: some babies quickly reach for flashing new toys while others hide behind their parent's legs. Children with high approach motivation head straight for the top of the monkey bars, lunge for a stranger's shiny keys, and beg to ride the craziest amusement park rides. In laboratory experiments, two-year-old children have been shown a strange new box with a hole in the side. Children who are low in approach shy away from the box entirely, whereas children high in approach instantly reach into the hole, sometimes trying to cram their whole toddler bodies into the box to more fully explore it. These biologically based tendencies show *stability,* the tendency to remain the same over time, such that our infantile tendencies to enjoy or dislike new sensations help form our adult personalities.

It is likely that high approach motivation is the basic core feature of Auguste's personality. The same motivation that would have made Auguste reach into a strange box at age two also drove him into untested bathyscapes and balloon cabins without hesitation. One type of high approach motivation is known as *sensation seeking*, which includes the tendency to seek out and enjoy thrills and adventures. In experiments, individuals who are high in sensation seeking show different physiological responses to unfamiliar sensations, such as strange sounds. When presented with a strange sound, most adults are startled and their heart rate accelerates. Adults who are high in sensation seeking, however, show a deceleration in heart rate when they hear a new sound, suggesting that they are calmly paying attention. While most of us would have had our hearts racing, as a sensation seeker, Auguste Piccard probably felt calm and attentive as he dangled thousands of feet above the ground in the pressurized cabin of his balloon.

Conclusion

Piccard's unique combination of social anxiety and sensation seeking made him just mad enough to attempt adventures with a balance of caution and reckless abandon. For example, Piccard gave his wife a dashing kiss on the hand before darting off to risk his own life in the stratosphere, but later promised to never attempt more extreme altitude balloon flights. Willing to keep his promise, but driven to explore, Piccard spent ten years designing his undersea vessel so he could explore the deep. Setting undersea depth records did not phase Auguste any more than his altitude records had; he kept diving and designing dive vessels until his death of natural causes at the age of seventy-eight.

Diagnosis

Axis I: Social anxiety disorder
Axis II: No diagnosis
Axis III: No diagnosis
Axis IV: Exposure to high altitudes and undersea pressure
Axis V: GAF = 90—superior functioning: mild anxiety; healthy relationships; sought out by others

PROFESSOR CALCULUS

(First appeared in Hergé's comic
Red Rackham's Treasure, 1944)

*"Please speak a bit louder.
I'm a little hard of hearing."*
—Professor Calculus

Nationality: French
Primary goals: Space travel
Hair: Around the sides, mostly
Likes: Roller skates
Dislikes: Billy clubs
Nickname: Mini-Piccard[1]
Honors: Knight Grand Cross of the Order of San Fernando
with Oak Leaves

1. This nickname was given by Hergé, the cartoonist who drew Calculus and claimed he had to be smaller than the real Piccard in order to fit more easily into a comic frame.

Genius:

Madness:

Introduction

The doddering Professor Cuthbert Calculus[2] is a beloved cartoon character from Hergé's Tintin comics, but he is directly modeled after the real-life scientist Auguste Piccard. Like his progenitor, the daring professor soars to the ends of Earth housed in various contrived metal contraptions. Calculus also sports Piccard's gutsy "science mullet" hairdo: completely bald on top with crazy curls around the back and sides—it's science up front and a party in the back. Calculus lived a life of adventure and intrigue, often leaving the laboratory behind to explore and eventually being kidnapped by Peruvians, Bordurians, and even those shifty Syldavians. The comic travails of the diminutive professor are testament to the real life of Auguste Piccard and a call to imagination for readers.

Portrait of a Scientist

Little is known about Calculus's family or educational background. He attended graduate school with Professor Hercules Tarragon, an expert on ancient America, but there is no information about what

2. In the original French versions of the Tintin comics, Calculus is named Professor Tournesol—the French word for sunflower. Literally, Tournesol means "turning sun," and the professor does seem to be drawn to the power of the sun and to all things astronomical. In his lifetime, Professor Calculus encounters spinning balls of lightning, travels to the moon, and nearly dies as a sacrifice to an Aztec sun god.

Calculus actually studied. It is likely that he excelled in a number of the physical sciences. Clearly, he has a strong understanding of mechanical engineering, as evinced by his invention of a number of complex machines, vehicles, and weapons. He also has extensive knowledge of nuclear chemistry and thermodynamics, which aided in his development of spacecraft. In *Destination Moon* (published in 1953), Cuthbert's nuclear-powered rocket succeeded in getting him and his companions to the moon and back. Calculus also seems to understand the workings of the sun and solar system; he is often seen using a small golden divining pendulum to find lost treasures (with arguable accuracy).

Enterprising Inventor

Although Cuthbert Calculus is primarily an explorer of the great unknown, he is also credited with many inventions great and small (e.g., the "wall bed," a device he created to save space in his labo-ratory). Among his other inventions include a somewhat dangerous machine for brushing clothing, an antidote to a chemical poison, the color television,[3] a lunar lander designed to explore the moon's surface, and even superpowered roller skates. Calculus's penchant for invention is sometimes a liability, as demonstrated when he is kidnapped by evil Bordurians eager to steal plans for his deadly ultrasonic weapon.

Shark submarine. Calculus is not merely a brilliant inventor, he is also a shrewd and somewhat sneaky businessman. In *Red Rack-ham's Treasure,* his understanding of the perils of the deep lead him to develop a sharkproof submarine for undersea exploration.

---

3. For information about the real inventor of the television, see Philo Farnsworth, pp. 171–81.

By constructing the small submarine to look like an actual shark, Calculus capitalizes on the efficient shape of a shark while protecting underwater adventurers from deadly shark versus submarine combat. Calculus was well prepared not only to build the device, but to sell it. Having never met young Tintin before, Calculus boldly approaches the reporter as he prepares for a treasure-hunting trip. When Tintin is not convinced that he needs the sharkproof submarine, Calculus simply breaks the machine into pieces and sneaks it aboard Tintin's ship. By the time he is discovered, it has become apparent that sharks are plentiful and Tintin will never reach the treasure without the shark-shaped submarine. Besides incidentally saving Tintin's life, Calculus also sells the submarine patent to the government for a substantial sum of money.

Philanthropic inventions. Many of Cuthbert Calculus's inventions are specifically designed to benefit mankind and solve problems of human suffering. In *Tintin and the Picaros,* he was awarded the prestigious (and verbose) award of "Knight Grand Cross of the Order of San Fernando with Oak Leaves" by General Alcazar, who was failing to overthrow General Tapioca because Tapioca kept dropping alcohol into Alcazar's camps and inebriating his soldiers. Calculus invented a pill that made alcohol taste horrible, thus saving Alcazar's men from liver disease and freeing them up to die in battle. In *Destination Moon,* Professor Calculus successfully developed another antidote, this time to "Formula Fourteen," a dangerous petroleum-based chemical that increased the explosive properties of crude oil and in humans caused massive hair growth, skin color changes, and uncomfortable production of green bubbles from the mouth (and possibly other orifices, as well). The development of these antidotes indicates that Calculus's inventions were not always strictly for personal gain.

Psychopathology: Attention Problems

Despite an array of amazing inventions, the professor demonstrates a number of symptoms that are consistent with a diagnosis of *attention-deficit/hyperactivity disorder* (*ADHD*), a disorder that is characterized by inattention, hyperactivity, and impulsivity.

Fails to listen when spoken to directly. Calculus often (in fact, almost always) fails to listen when spoken to directly—the most common symptom of inattention. However, it must be noted that this pronounced inattention may also be due to a profound hearing loss.

Easily distractible. ADHD is also characterized by easy distractibility, which Calculus demonstrates in a number of his comic appearances. On one occasion he becomes so caught up in his explanation of rocket fuels that he trips over electrical cords in a laboratory and smashes into a technician who is spray-painting a nuclear-powered rocket ship. In another instance, Calculus jumps up from a control panel and fails to remove his headphones before running off to attend to something.

Attention-related impairment. Although these moment-to-moment symptoms are entertaining and endearing in comic book characters, they often result in major life difficulties for real-life adults with ADHD. Adults with ADHD have difficulties planning ahead and managing their time; and their impulsivity makes them more likely to get into car accidents and engage in risky behaviors, including sexual risk taking and extreme sports. People who suffer from ADHD can also have difficulty forming intimate relationships, as they frequently overlook the details of social and relational obligations, such as returning phone calls. Calculus shows some of these difficulties. For example, he has trouble completing scientific projects (which are often seen laying half finished around his laboratory), and he is sometimes seen as a liability by his colleagues, who often attempt to leave him at home during high-risk adventures. Despite his inattentive symptoms, however, the professor always functions at a high enough level to accomplish ever more remarkable feats.

Physical Impairments

Although he won't admit it, much of Calculus's moment-to-moment inattention may be due to age-related *functional declines.* As we age, functional declines are common in a number of areas, including ambulation (i.e., walking) and balance, eyesight, and hearing. People vary in their perceptions of these declines, with some people overestimating their abilities and others underestimating them. Clearly, Professor Calculus tends to overestimate his functional abilities.

Functional decline in hearing. A number of humorous situations arise from Calculus's underestimation of his own deafness. In one instance, when he is about to be sacrificed to the Sun God along with Tintin and Captain Haddock, Calculus's hearing loss completely prevents him from grasping the gravity of the situation—he assumes that the deadly ritual is part of a historical drama. The professor's deafness may be entertaining for readers but it is quite dangerous for Calculus, especially because he does not believe that he is deaf. In *Destination Moon,* he tells Tintin that he is using a hand-held hearing aid instead of an ear piece because ear pieces are for deaf people. This denial of his true level of functional ability nearly costs him his life on multiple occasions, such as when he fails to hear fire alarms in the night and in one instance when he thinks that a bomb exploding is merely someone knocking at his door.

Functional decline in athleticism. Calculus's refusal to acknowledge his physical decline may be more understandable in light of the fact that he was not always elderly and clumsy. By his own report he was a great sportsman in his youth. In *Flight 714,* Calculus reveals that he used to practice *savate,* the French martial art of kickboxing. His extremely clumsy demonstration belies the expertise with which he practiced the sport in his youth. Although his physical prowess and agility clearly have diminished with age, his willingness to use his body in the pursuit of science has not. The elderly Cuthbert Calculus willingly tries riding the rocket-powered roller skates that he invented and does not hesitate to be the first to try piloting his shark submarine into the briny depths.

Calculus's Love Life: Surprising Attention to Detail

For a distracted scientist, Calculus pays surprising attention to the ladies. Many scientists like Calculus do not seem to be capable of love, as their attentions are solely focused on their work. This is not the case with Calculus, who seems quite adept at engaging in romantic gestures. For example, Calculus has been spotted courting at least one wealthy older woman. Bianca Castafiore is a famous opera singer whose piercing vocals bother everyone but Calculus. The professor thoughtfully presents the diva with a white rose (her name means "white chaste flower") following a concert in *The Castafiore Emerald.*

Calculus is no stranger to the world of fashion, either. In *Prisoners of the Sun,* Cuthbert compliments Captain Haddock on his hat and is later seen wearing an adorable red Peruvian hat complete with ear flaps. This sort of attention to detail outside of his scientific endeavors indicates that Calculus has a well-rounded personality and has been able to *generalize* this skill. When we generalize knowledge, we take what we know in one domain and apply it in another domain. Evidence indicates that Calculus has succeeded in generalizing his skill at attending to details in his scientific experiments to other areas, such as fashion and courtship.

Conclusion

Cuthbert Calculus lived a life of adventure and invention. He achieved moon landings, survived kidnappings, and developed advanced weapons (with advanced hearing loss). In addition to suffering from "Piccard-head," Calculus also struggled with symptoms of inattention and distractibility, which impaired his ability to finish all of the projects that he started. When Calculus did finish something, it was marvelous.

Diagnosis

Axis I: Attention deficit/hyperactivity disorder
Axis II: No diagnosis
Axis III: Hearing loss; Age-related functional declines
Axis IV: No diagnosis
Axis V: GAF + 80–slight impairment: easily excitable; works well with others

CAPTAIN NEMO

(First appeared in Jules Verne's novel *20,000 Leagues Under the Sea*, 1870)

"I am not what you call a civilized man, Professor. I have done away with society for reasons that seem good to me. Therefore I do not obey its laws."
—Captain Nemo

Nationality: Indian
Primary goals: Free the world from oppressive governments
Hair: Lots of it, mostly on his chin and eyebrows
Likes: Seaweed; smoking a pipe
Dislikes: Giant squid; the British
Hobbies: Dramatically playing the pipe organ through tears of unspeakable regret
Given name: Prince Dakkar
Nicknames: Captain No-One; Wizard of the Deep

Genius:

Madness:

Introduction

Captain Nemo is the mysterious explorer and scientist who appeared in Jules Verne's 1870 novel *20,000 Leagues Under the Sea* and its follow-up, *The Mysterious Island*. An outcast and renegade, Captain Nemo's very existence is largely unknown to the rest of the world, even as he travels the globe to support justified political revolutions. A mechanical genius, Nemo single-handedly designed and built the *Nautilus*, a submarine of stupendous proportions that is often mistaken for an undersea monster. In Latin, the word *Nemo* translates to "no-one," and Captain No-One is truly an enigmatic man who eschews life on land, preferring instead to explore the perilous depths of the ocean.

Portrait of a Scientist

On his deathbed, Captain Nemo divulges his surprising personal history, including details of his childhood. As the son of the Rajah of Bundelkund, Captain Nemo is Indian royalty—originally known as Prince Dakkar. Captain Nemo's powerful father sent him to Europe at the age of ten to receive a complete education, in hopes that he might return and lead the Indian nation (considered degraded and heathen) to a level equal to that of the nations of Western Europe. From age ten to thirty, Nemo excelled as a student, showing an incredible intellect and soaking up massive amounts of knowledge in science, literature, and art. In addition, he traveled to every corner of Europe, avoiding pleasures and focusing on satiating his hunger for knowledge. Throughout this period in his life, Nemo aspired to satisfy his father's (and nation's) hopes that he might become a great and powerful ruler to lead India into a new era of prosperity.

It is notable that even at a young age Nemo was capable of ignoring extraneous pleasures that were nearly unavoidable for a person of his rank and fortune. By all accounts, his social presence was extremely sought after and yet he paid no heed, being described as "grave" and "somber." Growing up in Europe as a privileged young man with the future of India on his shoulders may have contributed to Nemo's focus and determination during his youth, yet it may have also led to social isolation.[1]

Despite an expensive and well-rounded education—with success as an artist, a philosopher, and a statesman—Nemo chose to focus on science above all else. At this time in his life, Nemo possessed great status and a deep understanding of his studies, but the young man was still an innocent, inexperienced student. The same relations that afforded Nemo these educational opportunities also cost him his innocence.

Psychopathology

After studying in Europe, Captain Nemo returned to his homeland of Bundelkund in 1849. Soon after, he married a noble Indian lady and they had two daughters. But domestic bliss was not to last for the young scientist, as the British conquest of India was under way. In 1857, the people of India revolted against their British occu-

---

1. Rocket scientist Jack Parsons received a similarly opulent upbringing and was socially ostracized by his classmates as a result.

piers. As the nephew of Tippoo Sahib, the ruler of the Kingdom of Mysore, Captain Nemo was inextricably drawn into battle against British troops led by Arthur Wellesley, the first Duke of Wellington.

During this time, Nemo became a soldier and fought in the front infantry ranks against the British. He was wounded ten times out of twenty bloody engagements. It was also during this time that Nemo lost his wife and children. As the rebellion dragged on and the Indian troops were defeated time after time, Captain Nemo behaved with less and less concern for his own safety. By the tenth battle (and tenth wound), it was clear to those around him that Nemo was actively seeking his own death. A psychologist of the late 1800s, Sigmund Freud, identified this human desire to return to an original inanimate (or dead) state and named it the *death drive*. After the dust settled, the Indian revolutionaries had been soundly defeated.

Post-traumatic stress symptoms. Since the 1800s, there have been more wars and more study of the psychological problems of veterans. What was originally known as shell shock has now been identified as a collection of post-traumatic stress symptoms that are a relatively common occurrence for men and women involved in direct combat or personal traumatic events such as assault, rape, or witnessing the death of family members. Post-traumatic stress symptoms even occur under lesser circumstances, such as when an individual is threatened with death or serious injury and feels intense fear, helplessness, or horror. The fact is that simply being exposed to insane situations can upset an individual's mental balance. Some post-traumatic stress symptoms include

⚡ *Re-experiencing symptoms,* such as distressing and intrusive thoughts, recurrent dreams, or flashbacks of reliving the event

⚡ *Avoidant symptoms,* including efforts to avoid thinking about the event, avoidance of activities and places related to the event, and feelings of detachment or dissociation with reality

⚡ *Persistent increased arousal symptoms,* such as being easily startled by noises, having trouble sleeping, and being hypervigilant

Post-traumatic stress disorder. Psychological diagnosis depends on exactly how and when the above symptoms appear. When symptoms cause distress during the month following a trauma, the individual is diagnosed with acute stress disorder. When these symptoms persist for longer than a month, a diagnosis of *post-traumatic stress disorder* is often appropriate. In Nemo's case, the trauma of fighting a losing war that was his destiny to win and being injured repeatedly was compounded by the loss of his family, and his symptoms in response to these traumatic stressors lasted well over a month. In fact, the post-traumatic stress disorder resulting from war and loss sent Nemo into an anguished and avoidant lifelong undersea journey focused on revenge against anyone he considered a tyrant.

As a prince who had fought openly against the British, a price was put upon Nemo's head immediately after the war. He barely managed to escape to his remote mountain homeland of Bundelkund. Defeated, devastated, and alone in the world, Nemo developed a deep disgust and hatred for humankind itself. He assembled a great many of his most noble countrymen and disappeared from his homeland forever. Perhaps melodramatically, at this point Prince Dakkar renamed himself Captain Nemo—no one—and disappeared beneath the waves.[2] This could certainly be a symptom of *avoidance* related to post-traumatic stress disorder, as

2. Dr. *No* was also melodramatically self-named.

living beneath the sea certainly helped Nemo avoid the activities, places, and people who would have reminded him of war had he remained in Bundelkund.

Nemo at Peace: Isolation and Secrecy

When an adult individual isolates him- or herself and withdraws from mainstream society, it may be due to external situational factors or due to the internal traits of the individual. In the field of personality psychology these are often referred to as *state and trait* factors. Having spent several decades undersea, it is clear that the affairs of the above-ground world meant little to Captain Nemo. In fact, he designed and built the *Nautilus* in secret on a deserted island specifically because he wished to flee the barbarism of the human race. Captain Nemo was a loner during his childhood and he did not want to have any part of the wars and persecution that he perceived as inevitable on the surface.

Thus, a combination of state and trait characteristics probably led to his extreme behaviors. The extreme trauma following the death of Nemo's family likely contributed to his isolation, as did his personality trait of *introversion*. One of the fundamental traits of personality is introversion, the tendency to gain pleasure from one's inner or mental life, as opposed to *extraversion*, the tendency to gain pleasure from interactions with other people. Even before the war, Nemo preferred to study alone and did not take part in many social gatherings. Regardless of what exact combination of state and trait factors led to Captain Nemo's isolation, it was certainly an abnormal and unusual behavior, although somewhat common among mad scientists.[3]

3. Oliver Heaviside, Victor Frankenstein, and Seth Brundle also chose to isolate themselves from human contact in an extreme manner.

Scientific Accomplishments

Like Marie Curie,[4] the traumatized Captain Nemo forthwith devoted himself to the study of science. In particular, Nemo focused on oceanography and the design of submersibles. On a deserted Pacific island, he built a dockyard to house an ever-more-complicated submarine prototype. Based on his own designs, Nemo and his followers built an electrically powered submarine capable of moving at great speeds while keeping its occupants warm and safe. This required an understanding of ballasts, propeller systems, and the buoyancy of gases. Eventually, Nemo succeeded in designing the most luxurious and mysterious undersea vessel ever built.[5] Dubbed the *Nautilus*, the submersible was so far ahead of its time that the scientifically stunted American Navy considered it to be nothing less than a sea monster.

In addition to the *Nautilus*, Nemo invented a variety of accessories necessary for a life of solitude beneath the waves. Underwater diving suits allowed Nemo and his crew to leave the submarine and trudge across the sea floor on hunting expeditions. As the sleek suits automatically expelled impure air, the occupants clutched underwater rifles powered by compressed air cartridges and stayed on the lookout for sharks, the "tigers of the deep." At other times, the nineteenth-century aquanauts would harvest food from the bountiful ocean or raid the wrecked hulls of sunken ships for huge troves of invaluable treasure. Nemo's wealth, scientific prowess, and avoidant coping behavior allowed him to shun the surface entirely, exploring the undersea world and being sustained by it for years at a time.

---

4. After the loss of her husband and scientific partner, Marie Curie devoted herself to science with newfound vigor and isolated herself in the laboratory for months at a time.
5. In 1870, Nemo's fictional undersea design was years ahead of Auguste Piccard's real bathyscape design, which launched in the 1930s.

Empathy and Philanthropy

Despite his isolation from landlubbers, Nemo demonstrated significant empathy and philanthropy toward his fellow humans and a willingness to interact in the affairs of those he viewed as oppressed. Captain Nemo occasionally delivered portions of his bountiful undersea treasure to deserving humans on the surface. The history of British invasion and exploitation of India may be a large factor in his unflagging support for those who are under oppression by military or government powers. At one point, Nemo declared that the mission of the *Nautilus* and its crew is to travel the world battling injustice and cruelty, specifically slavery. Thus, his philanthropic gifts were almost always targeted toward humans engaging in justified revolution. For example, he delivered valuable treasures scavenged from sea-bottom wrecks to Cretan soldiers resisting a Turkish invasion. Unfortunately, this sort of behavior did not always please the British and American governments, who eventually came to view Nemo as a vigilante and a danger to society.

In 1867, a group of three men were pursuing the *Nautilus* aboard the U.S. frigate *Abraham Lincoln*, seeking to capture Captain Nemo. These men, including a Professor Aronnax, fell off the frigate and into the sea. Rather than let them drown, Nemo showed compassion and took his enemies aboard as prisoners, keeping them comfortable and safe but against their will.[6] When the men escaped several months later during a terrible storm, Nemo assumed they were dead and never thought of them again.[7]

The Captain also saved the life of a pearl diver who nearly

---

6. Dr. No demonstrates similar kindness to prisoners, keeping James Bond and Honey Ryder in luxurious quarters.

7. Unknown to Nemo, these men live to tell the tale of *20,000 Leagues Under the Sea,* effectively making Nemo into a famous character worldwide without his knowledge.

drowned, rescued a number of castaways from certain death, and covertly kept an eye on those in trouble at sea in case his rescue services were needed. In addition, Captain Nemo demonstrated the greatest care and empathy for his crew, bravely fighting off a giant squid and effectively keeping his cool in the face of great danger.

Conclusion

Captain Nemo likely suffered from symptoms of post-traumatic stress disorder following traumatic experiences associated with war and the death of his family. He coped with this stress by isolating himself under the sea and throwing himself into his underwater scientific endeavors. Nemo also demonstrated levels of empathy that were higher than what is typically seen in mad scientists, giving undersea treasures to those fighting oppression around the world. After decades at sea, all of Nemo's trusted comrades succumbed to old age. At the age of sixty, Nemo found himself alone on the *Nautilus* with all of his crew dead of old age. He navigated the fantastic ship to a hidden dock and parked to await his own death. Ultimately, Captain Nemo was a conflicted hero—a genius who was tortured by fate and died without ever fulfilling his destiny.

Diagnosis

Axis I: Post-traumatic stress disorder; Bereavement
Axis II: No diagnosis
Axis III: No diagnosis
Axis IV: Lives in unusual conditions (submarine)
Axis V: GAF = 50—serious symptoms: social isolation; transient suicidal preoccupation

COMMUNICATED WITH SPACE ALIENS

The top tier, most brilliant mad scientists are gifted with brains so powerful that it is no surprise that they may be hard to handle. After all, driving a moped is easier than steering a rocket-powered racing bike. The brainiest of mad scientists may make extravagant claims about the origins of their most amazing ideas, but who among us can say what is or isn't possible to those operating in the lofty realm of superintelligence?

This section considers a group of mad scientists who were convinced they were communicating with beings from outer space. These conferences were of questionable origin, but have nevertheless resulted in wondrous technological artifacts. The question remains: Did this incredible information come from advanced beings from outer space, or from insightful voices speaking from the inner depths of the human mind?

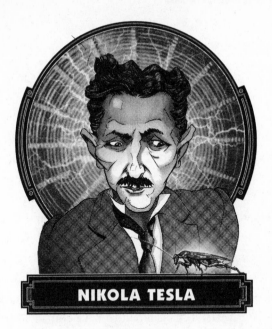

NIKOLA TESLA

(1856–1943)

"My invention requires a large plant, but once it is established, it will be possible to destroy anything, men or machines, approaching within a radius of 200 miles."
—Nikola Tesla

Nationality: Serbian American
Primary goals: Free electricity; germ-free society
Hair: Parted, greased
Number of patents: 212
Likes: Water; pigeons
Dislikes: Germs; Thomas Edison
Nickname: The Electrical Genius

Genius:

Madness:

Introduction

Nikola Tesla is a wholly original and real-life mad scientist. Although he died before the transistor was invented, Tesla used his formidable mind as we use computers today; he designed, constructed, and tested all of his inventions using only the power of mental concentration. Without making a single sketch, Tesla then built precise working models of his electrifying inventions. Tesla's intelligence was sharpened by his intense powers of concentration, which had both blessed and tortured him beginning in childhood. In the extreme case, Tesla appears to have suffered from symptoms of *obsessive-compulsive disorder* (*OCD*), especially later in life. He spent much of his life working obsessively and in solitude; interacting with ordinary humans seemed difficult for him. Perhaps this is why, in his later years, Tesla claimed to have contacted the superior intelligences of beings from the planet Venus. Despite his eccentricities, or possibly because of them, Nikola Tesla was able to use his mind to improve the lives of billions of human beings.

Portrait of a Scientist

There is substantial evidence that, as a child, Nikola's intelligence quotient (IQ) would likely have fallen in the "very superior" range (at least two standard deviations above the mean, above the 95th percentile). There are several reported anecdotes that exemplify his precociousness. When he was only five years old, Nikola informed his father that he was going to harness the power of water. His resulting invention was a water-powered egg beater. By age nine, Nikola's egg beater had been upgraded so that it was powered by the motion of captured bugs. The next year, Tesla was solving math equations with such amazing speed that his teachers suspected him of cheating. Nikola performed additional tests under the close watch of his parents and teachers, proving that he was a child prodigy. Little Nikola's technological imagination was in full swing as a child—he believed that someday it would be possible to photograph thoughts.

While Tesla's remarkable cognitive abilities were certainly inherited from his parents (Nikola's father knew the entire Bible by heart and his mother spoke four languages), his inherent brightness was enhanced by nearly obsessive concentration and intense motivation. It is possible that this intensity resulted in part because of the tragic death of his older brother, which occured when Tesla was five. In the aftermath of this tragedy, it is reported that the young Nikola became determined to be as good and as smart as his older brother had been. As a five-year-old child, Tesla demonstrated the ability to sustain his attention for unusually long time spans, spending hours at a time on his projects and inventions. Tesla also had exceptional visual memory abilities; he could hold the idea of a machine or invention in his mind and "test it" through visual rotation and by visualizing the machine in motion.

Although clearly a brilliant child, Tesla also demonstrated eccentric and bizarre early behaviors. He was overly sensitive to certain sounds and physical sensations and could barely tolerate loud noises such as a train going by. These sorts of symptoms are often seen in children with a diagnosis of *autism* (a developmental disorder that impairs communication and social skills), although autistic disorders were virtually unknown at the time Tesla was a child.

Tesla graduated from the Serbian equivalent of a four-year high school program in just three years. Then, at the age of seventeen, he exposed himself to cholera. Why would a genius intentionally expose himself to a deadly disease? Tesla was simply avoiding required military service so that he could continue his studies. Though Tesla had largely recovered by the time a military doctor arrived to examine him, he managed to appear weak enough to receive a certificate of disability. This "critical illness" allowed him to secretly return to his studies after a year of rest (during which Tesla read novels, learned to play billiards with his father, and meticulously memorized the majority of the contents of his local library).

At the Polytechnic Institute in Graz, Austria, and at Prague University, Tesla continued his quest for knowledge and conclusively proved himself a nerd. He regularly woke at 3:00 a.m. to work on his most difficult homework problems (after sleeping only four hours). During the first year of college, Tesla passed nine subject exams when most students only took five subjects. A letter from the dean of Prague University to Tesla's parents declared that "Your son is a star of the first magnitude." In his free time, Tesla organized the first intercollegiate activity in which a team from one university would challenge a team from another university: chess.

Psychopathology: Irrational Fears

There is some evidence that, as he grew older, Tesla may have suffered from *OCD*. It is likely that the same mental focus and intensity that helped him accomplish complex scientific tasks and calculations contributed to his obsessive tendencies. Tesla's likely OCD impaired him in many domains, especially in social interactions; his obsessions included phobias (fears) of dirt and germs, as well as an intense focus on the number three and on completing calculations about things in his immediate environment.

Mental obsessions are often associated with behavioral compulsions performed according to rigid rules. Tesla felt driven to perform repetitive behaviors, such as doing everything in sets of three. For example, after walking around a block once, Tesla would feel compelled to do so two more times. He also preferred to dine alone, due to his meticulous compulsion to clean his plates and silverware with eighteen (divisible by three) napkins before a meal. (Afterward, he calculated the cubic contents of all the food on his plate before eating.) Individuals with extreme obsessions and compulsions often have difficulty maintaining relationships, as their idiosyncratic habits impair normal routines and can be time consuming and embarrassing.

Although an obstacle to social relations, Tesla's obsessions also fueled some of his scientific ideas. In a 1915 article he predicted that electricity would lead to the purging of microbes, insects, and rodents from Earth. He also predicted that electrical "baths" would be in every home and would rid the body of dust or other small particles and that municipalities would adopt electric dust absorbers and devices to sterilize air, food, and water. Tesla was clearly interested in using technology to alleviate his own obsessional problems.

Adult Relationships

Although he was close to his family, Tesla had very few intimate relationships as an adult. He never married or had children. Tesla's obsessions and his phobia of germs probably contributed to this. It is reported that Tesla did not like touching hair or shaking hands and thus avoided human contact. He frequently worked alone on his inventions, turning things over and over in his mind. During a period of unemployment as an engineer, Tesla took a job digging ditches. During this job he did develop friendships with his fellow day laborers. Although he seemed capable of developing friendships, Tesla rarely sought or cultivated these relationships.

Tesla had particular difficulties interacting with authority figures, especially his employers, undoubtedly because of his superior understanding of the electrical systems he was working on. He faced constant frustration because his mind held perfect designs for futuristic machines that did not yet exist. Instead of being able to freely create his designs, he was forced to work instead for people who could not even comprehend them. Tesla preferred to work alone because he could not slow down to wait for "lesser men" (including Thomas Edison). At times, these "creative differences" would lead to Tesla's dismissal.

In his later years, Tesla became even more socially isolated. He began to spend part of each day methodically feeding pigeons and caring for injured birds in his Waldorf Astoria apartment. Despite his irrational fear of germs, he was often seen in the park with pigeons covering his arms (he even had a favorite white pigeon that visited his apartment window).

Scientific Achievements

An undisputed genius, Tesla pounded out over two hundred radically new inventions. Half a century after his death, more than one hundred of Tesla's patents were still in active use by countless millions.

Tesla's creations included a host of brilliant (and by now mundane) inventions, including the arc light, alternating current motors, and systems for transmitting electricity and lighting homes. He is most famous for the "Tesla coil," designed to step up electrical voltages at high frequencies—a required step for propagating waves with antennas. It is argued that Tesla should be credited with the invention of the radio, too. In fact, his system of oscillating, tuned circuits did make the radio possible. Tesla also introduced the concept of the microwave oven. He possessed a strong intuitive understanding of electricity and radio waves, which was no doubt enabled by his ability to envision completely functional machines in motion.

Tesla proposed many ideas about power that were fairly accurate, and some others that were a bit outlandish. For example, he understood that wireless transmission of energy was possible but did not recognize that there would be limits on how much energy could be transmitted through the air. Tesla envisioned a huge tower that would distribute free energy to everyone on Earth by bouncing current off the ionosphere, but he did not realize that this technique would not generate sufficiently high currents for running things like lights and appliances (although it does work for AM radio). Tesla also envisioned this device as a giant weapon, which he attempted to sell for defense purposes.[1] Tesla also believed that one could use this energy to change Earth's weather patterns, which scientists today believe is impossible. Tesla's understanding of the ionosphere and wireless energy transmission was certainly far ahead of his time, but his visions sometimes exceeded the constraining realities of the physical world.

The Alien Incident

Tesla's reputation as a living "mad" scientist was cemented by the so-called alien incident. His mental faculties were called into question by much of the scientific establishment after he declared he was receiving messages from inhabitants of either Mars or Venus over his radio-receiving equipment. He believed there was life in the universe besides our own and was intensely interested in finding ways to communicate with other inhabitants of our solar system. Unfortunately, Tesla never convinced other scientists that he had detected signs of intelligent extraterrestrials.

1. Like Dr. Evil, Tesla requested exorbitant sums of money from government officials, negotiating with the prime minister of Great Britain for 30 million U.S. dollars (about a half billion dollars in today's market) in exchange for a defense ray machine. These negotiations failed, and there is no known prototype of Tesla's "death ray."

Conclusion

The very characteristics that made Tesla "mad" may have contributed the most to his scientific genius. His ability to concentrate and focus on mental images was no doubt related to both his obsessive-compulsive tendencies *and* his skill at envisioning amazingly complex electrical machines in action. Tesla's life illustrates the fine line that exists between genius and madness.

Diagnosis

Axis I: Obsessive-compulsive disorder; Psychotic disorder not otherwise specified (alien hallucinations)

Axis II: No diagnosis

Axis III: No diagnosis

Axis IV: Social isolation

Axis V: GAF = 60–moderate symptoms: conflicts with coworkers; impairment in reality testing

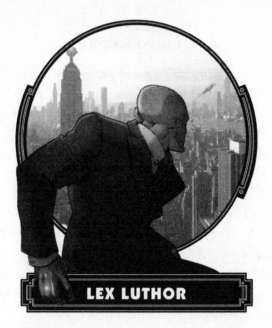

LEX LUTHOR

(First appeared in Action comics, 1940)

"Just an ordinary man—but with the brain of a super genius!"
—Lex Luthor, *Action Comics* No. 19, 1940

Nationality: Lexorian
Primary goals: Enslave Earth, universe
Arch-enemy: Superman
Current residence: Metropolis
Favorite materials: Kryptonite; lead
Education: Master's degree in "Science," MIT
Heroes: Atilla the Hun; Al Capone; Benedict Arnold
Hobby: Philanthropy

Genius:

Madness:

Introduction

Lex Luthor is a supervillain, a super genius, and one hell of a guy. Although Luthor's scientific genius may be fueled by an intense desire to destroy Superman (his arch-enemy), in his spare time Luthor is an accomplished philanthropist. A man of extremes, Lex Luthor exhibits traits of both *obsessive-compulsive personality disorder*[1] and narcissistic personality disorder. Additionally, it is probable that he suffers from a manic mood disorder. Although this manic mood disorder is likely to be biologically based, Luthor's problematic personality traits appear to be rooted in events that occurred during his adolescence. The combination of obsessive traits, narcissism, and mania make Lex Luthor a force to be reckoned with—he is on a never-ending quest for economic power, world respect and idolatry, and all-out domination of the universe.

Portrait of a Scientist

Luthor was raised by his biological parents in the town of Smallville alongside his future nemesis Superman (conveniently known then as Superboy). As a child, Luthor faced severe economic hardship, living with his family in a neighborhood called Suicide Slum.[2] Luthor has one known sibling, a sister named Lena Thorul, who had powers of extrasensory perception. Both of Luthor's parents perished in a suspicious car accident when he was just fourteen years old. The young Lex (and not his sister) became the sole beneficiary of a valuable insurance policy, which he immediately used to fund his education at MIT.

1. Obsessive-compulsive personality disorder is *not* the same diagnosis as obsessive-compulsive disorder (OCD). For a description of OCD, see p. 65.
2. The mathematician Oliver Heaviside was born into a similar slum.

It is unclear whether Luthor was at all responsible for the death of his parents, but it is a definite possibility. The fourteen-year-old Lex was certainly intelligent enough to plan and execute an "accident" that would not have been detected by the authorities. Unfortunately, we know little about Luthor's relationship with his parents before they died. However, given what we know about his subsequent relationships, a plausible hypothesis is that Luthor resented growing up in the slums and blamed his parents for the fact that he did not have the advantages that many of his peers in Smallville enjoyed. Luthor may have felt as though he deserved better. Even if he was not directly responsible for his parents' deaths, Luthor sent himself to MIT, an opportunity that might not have been available without the economic advantage provided by his parents' untimely demise.

Lex Luthor's bitterness toward Superman began during his tragic adolescence. Initially, Superboy and Lex admired each other's abilities—Superboy was impressed with Lex's genius and Lex was amazed by Superboy's powers. Lex even saved Superboy's life by disposing of a kryptonite rock and Superboy later built Lex a laboratory. But this friendship was not meant to last. One day Superboy put out a fire in Lex's laboratory with his super-breath, but inadvertently blew hazardous chemicals onto Lex's fiery-red coiffure. Luthor's luxurious mane of hair was subsequently lost in the explosion and Luthor blamed Superman for making him permanently bald. And thus began a lifelong enmity.

By all accounts, Luthor was extremely intelligent as a child. He began studies at MIT by age fourteen and astounded his professors with a series of brilliant inventions. After three years, Luthor graduated with a Master's Degree in Science. However, his educational accomplishments did not earn him personal relationships. During this period, Luthor developed a pattern of resenting others in close relationships and blaming others for his problems. The adolescent

Luthor's narcissistic sense of *entitlement* (feeling of a unique right or claim to something) began during his college years, as he felt entitled to a better childhood. Likewise, Luthor illogically believed that he was entitled to keep his full head of red hair, blaming Superboy for what was obviously an accident. Often, such feelings of entitlement are developed by an individual to compensate for an underlying *low self-esteem* (feeling unworthy or lacking in genuine pride in oneself). Ultimately, Luthor came to resent others for a multitude of reasons, including for trying to help him. Superman nobly bore the brunt of resentment from the young, bald Luthor, which in turn fueled the adult development of Luthor's obsessive-compulsive personality characteristics.

Psychopathology

Lex Luthor exhibits symptoms of a manic mood disorder, as well as some characteristic traits of obsessive-compulsive and narcissistic personality disorders. The most prominent symptoms are listed below:

Obsessive-compulsive preoccupation with details, lists, and organization. In his private fortress, known as Luthor's Lair, Lex maintains a Reminder Room, which is solely devoted to the storage of past calendars. These orderly calendars are conspicuously displayed, and days on the calendars have been meticulously crossed out. Luthor claims that these calendars help remind him of the time in his life he has spent imprisoned because of Superman.

Obsessive-compulsive devotion to work and productivity. There is no doubt that Luthor is excessively devoted to his life's work: the task of destroying Superman. In fact, his devotion is so great that it is difficult to imagine how he has time to run his exceedingly profitable corporations, manage his political career, or host swank dinner parties—much less eat or sleep.

Narcissistic grandiose sense of self-importance. Luthor's sense of self-importance is easily seen in the names of his creations, as nearly every invention is named after Lex. For instance, the LEXO-SKEL SUIT 5000 is a clever pairing of the words "Lex" and "exoskeleton," and the Lexwing aircraft also bears his name. Although Luthor's companies employ large numbers of people, they are all housed under an umbrella company called LexCorp.

Narcissistic preoccupation with fantasies of unlimited success, money, and power. Luthor is mad for power and success. In fact, there is no time when he is not scheming about ways to exercise more control over the world, and ultimately, the universe.

Manic mood disorder. Lex Luthor's obsessive-compulsive and narcissistic behaviors may be fueled by an underlying mood disorder consisting of recurrent manic episodes. Despite his constant failures, Luthor demonstrates unusually high levels of energy when it comes to plotting Superman's destruction. Mania is also frequently marked by an inflated self-esteem or grandiosity (which could partially account for Luthor's belief that he alone deserves to rule the universe). Manic episodes also lead to increases in goal-directed activity and recurrent episodes might correspond with Luthor's repeated rallying for a seemingly endless series of attempts to take Superman's life.

Adult Relationship with Superman

In adulthood, Luthor focuses nearly all of his evil energies on eradicating Superman, as Superman is the only thing standing in the way of world domination. In fact, the two men have met personally in battle hundreds of times. Luthor probably feels as though Superboy's original betrayal has continued into adulthood as Superman continues to thwart Luthor's malevolent plans. Luthor's narcissistic sense of entitlement leads to jealousy of Superman's success in Metropolis. In stark contrast to Superman, people do not naturally like and respect Luthor, and in order to achieve the high level of respect that Luthor feels he deserves, he must buy it. Obsessing about the fundamental unfairness of this situation, Luthor probably translates his intense desire for respect and power into clever attacks on Superman.

Notable Accomplishments

Aliases and alternate identities. Luthor has succeeded in adopting alternate personae as needed in his fiendish schemes. These identities enable him to maintain his antisocial behaviors and have included Carlyle Allerton, Mr. Smith, Professor Clyde, Professor Guthrie, The Defender, Luthor the Noble, and the nefarious Zytal. While these alter-egos have been unmasked by Superman, there may be other aliases that Luthor has secretly maintained.

Economic and social power. Lex Luthor's villainous career has been extremely profitable, likely motivated by his mania. He has been listed in *Forbes'*, "Top 10 Richest Fictional Men." Luthor was a self-made billionaire by age twenty, primarily through patenting his inventions and selling them to the military. He manages to buy power and influence in Metropolis and, in fact, is one of the city's greatest benefactors. His companies employ no less than two-thirds of the workforce of Metropolis.

Outstanding philanthropy. Exactly what motivates Lex Luthor's philanthropy is unclear. What *is* clear is that he has donated millions of dollars to Metropolis over the years, including funding for parks, foundations, and medical charities. It is interesting to note that, despite being a notorious supervillain, Luthor once saved an entire planet and its inhabitants from destruction. This planet made him a hero and the inhabitants renamed the planet Lexor. Unfortunately, even this good deed came to a bad end at Luthor's own hand, as he accidentally demolished Lexor (along with his own Lexorian wife and child) in battle with Superman. It is likely that grandiose acts of generosity are rooted in Luthor's underlying low self-esteem and intense desire to be liked and respected by others, regardless of the cost.

Scientific Achievements

Lex Luthor is arguably the greatest renegade scientist of all time. In addition to creating flying cars, rocket jetpacks, and space craft, Luthor has invented dozens of ridiculously destructive weapons for the military. One such weapon, the previously mentioned LEXO-SKEL SUIT 5000, is a protective robotic exoskeleton for soldiers. (An attempt by Luthor to sell these suits to "Kaznian" terrorists was foiled by Superman.) Luthor's general science degree seems to have served him well; his strong grasp of chemistry allowed him to manufacture *luthorite,* a synthetic version of the naturally occurring element *kryptonite.* He also succeeded in designing a device to summon beings from the fourth dimension.[3]

Ironically, it is Luthor's arch-enemy who has inspired the most

---

3. Similar experiments were met with failure by Jack Parsons, a famed rocket scientist and occultist.

innovative of his creations. Given that Superman's X-ray vision poses a huge obstacle to the successful completion of Luthor's diabolical inventions, Luthor has been forced to create clever secret bases, many of which are lined with lead to debilitate Superman's X-ray vision. These secretive retreats have included a farmhouse near Metropolis, abandoned factories, an electronics firm in Metropolis, a secret mountaintop laboratory and fortress, a lead-lined subterranean hideout under a grassy hill, an ancient glass-enclosed city, a giant spaceship laboratory, a complex of buildings held in the air by a huge dirigible, and a lair on a man-made meteor floating in outer space.

Luthor has also given birth to genius inventions when he has applied his scientific acumen to his criminal endeavors. These creations have included a vault blaster, a money magnet, an earthquake maker, and an atomic death ray.

Conclusion

Despite a lifetime of accomplishments, Lex Luthor has never realized his simple dream of dominating the world and subsequently the universe. Fortunately for Superman, Luthor's "madness" may contribute to his inability to achieve his goals. In fact, individuals with obsessive-compulsive personality disorder often become so focused on details and goal setting they have difficulty following through with their plans and will sometimes execute them poorly. Although Luthor's mania-fueled intensity keeps him focused on seeking Superman's demise, it no doubt causes him to miss other opportunities to gain power. The citizens of Metropolis can thank the predictability of Luthor's obsessions (and Superman, of course) for keeping Luthor's power in check.

Diagnosis

Axis I: Manic episodes, Moderate severity, Recurrent

Axis II: Narcissistic personality disorder; Obsessive-compulsive personality disorder

Axis III: No diagnosis

Axis IV: No diagnosis

Axis V: GAF = 100–superior functioning: rich; famous; as evil as he wants to be

PERFORMED
HUMAN EXPERIMENTS

It's a sad fact that superior intelligence and morality do not necessarily go hand in hand. And that goes double for mad scientists. Addicted to discovery, a mad scientist can sometimes look at other people and see experiments waiting to happen instead of fellow human beings with thoughts, feelings, and the strong desire not to be dissected. But like a fire that is out of control, a mad scientist's untamed curiosity can sometimes grow to consume everything in its path—including innocent test subjects.

This section unearths the exploits of a group of mad scientists who were willing to risk the health and sanity of everyday people in order to fuel their scientific endeavors. With scalpels, electroshock generators, and walls echoing with victims' screams—

these doctors surrendered to their most primitive curiosity and ruthlessly explored the deepest animal nature of humanity. Some of these mad scientists exhibit mild mood disorders, while others are entrenched in nearly immutable personality flaws. In either case, they show us that in the search for scientific truth, sometimes the needs of the little people are sacrificed to great minds.

DR. MOREAU

(First appeared in H. G. Wells's novel *The Island of Dr. Moreau*, 1896)

"Do you know what it means to feel like God?"
—Dr. Moreau

Nationality: British
Primary goals: Making the perfect human-animal hybrid; spreading suntan lotion evenly over entire body
Voice: Lispy
Likes: Classical music; mammals
Dislikes: Public scrutiny; bright sunlight
Hobbies: Vivisection; playing the grand piano
Favorite drink: Brandy
Best known for: "The Moreau Horrors"; making a sexy puma-lady

Genius:

Madness:

Introduction

This frightening recluse was popularized in H. G. Wells's 1896 novel, *The Island of Dr. Moreau*, and appeared later in several movies of the same name. Generally characterized as an overweight hermit with a strange skin condition, Dr. Moreau's most identifiable trait is a complete willingness to go beyond the normal limits of research and directly into the realm of playing God. A scientific genius and moral washout, Dr. Moreau ignores the judgments of his fellow humans and successfully creates a new race of physically malformed, intelligent creatures. Flawed as they are, even Moreau's monstrous race of human-animal hybrids are capable of recognizing that the doctor is not all powerful. Blinded by his delusions of grandeur, Dr. Moreau is eventually judged by those he has created—and deemed unworthy.

Portrait of a Scientist

Dr. Moreau originally conducted his research in Britain at a legitimate academic institution. However, the morality of his work came into question after a journalist found a horribly mutilated dog in Moreau's laboratory, starting a scandal known as "Moreau's Horrors." Dr. Moreau immediately lost his university job and research funding after officials discovered that the dog was the subject of a horrific dissection. The journalist created a pamphlet documenting Moreau's unappetizing research methods. After the cruel and painful nature of his experiments became public knowledge, Moreau was forced to make some tough decisions.

With his career ruined, Dr. Moreau chose to continue his research outside the fetters of the scientific establishment. Other mad scientists in similar situations have chosen differently, either apologizing for their actions and continuing work with colleagues[1] or forcing the overall scientific establishment into moral alignment.[2] Dr. Moreau, however, chose to escape to an isolated island in order to continue his work. There, he set up an admirably secluded laboratory.[3] With eight square miles of volcanic tropical paradise surrounded by bountiful coral reefs, the island was perfect. In addition to building a home suitable for relaxed island living, Moreau set up an extensive complex of cages for housing his subjects and a state-of-the-art, sanitary operating room. He recruited a loyal research assistant and prepared to continue his research.

This course of action indicates that Dr. Moreau was likely suffering from a delusional disorder, specifically of the grandiose type. Individuals with this disorder hold untrue beliefs that their own knowledge or worth is much higher than it actually is. In Dr. Moreau's case, it seems that his belief in the value of his own work was strong enough to override the opinions of his scientific contemporaries and the public at large. Dr. Moreau was possessed by a senselessly confident feeling that it was his destiny to continue this abominable line of research. With this knowledge, it is no surprise that Dr. Moreau went to extreme lengths to continue his work.

1. The psychologist Stanley Milgram later expressed remorse over experiments in which he fooled experimental subjects into believing they had shocked innocent people to death.
2. As president of the Academy of Agricultural Sciences, Trofim Lysenko ensured agreement by having his detractors imprisoned, tortured, and killed.
3. Lex Luthor had even more secluded laboratories, including mountain and farmhouse lairs.

Scientific Accomplishments

Dr. Moreau possessed an amazing knowledge of genetic science for his time. In addition to being able to read medical textbooks in their original Latin and Greek, Dr. Moreau had mastered a wide range of advanced surgical techniques and held a position of prominence as a physiology researcher. He focused on creating hybrid creatures, something people at the end of the nineteenth century feared enormously.[4] He also researched blood transfusions and cancerous growths. The doctor was also an expert at *vivisection,* the dissection and surgical testing of animals. (Questionably, Dr. Moreau was not above vivisecting living animals to understand the operation of ongoing biological functions.)

On the island, Dr. Moreau successfully vivisected monkeys, hogs, dogs, leopards, oxen, and pumas and mutilated them into human shapes. Worse yet, he combined dangerous creatures together, like hyena and swine. His experimentation was careless, irresponsible, and unnecessarily cruel. Although many of his hybrid creations did not survive beyond the operating table, Dr. Moreau's surgical techniques improved over time (as did his success rates). Eventually, the island was populated by dozens of hideously deformed mutant experiments-gone-wrong with barely tamed animal desires. Dr. Moreau and his assistants were essentially trapped in their homes at night, hoping that the rabbits they had released onto the island provided enough food for the dangerous man-beasts.

It is unclear exactly what sorts of surgical techniques Moreau used, but it seems likely that he managed to surgically combine creatures and then use blood transfusion and other techniques to merge the creatures at the genetic level, while sidestepping the issues of foreign body rejection. Moreau claimed that no humans

4. See Dr. Victor Frankenstein, pp. 99–108.

were harmed in the creation of his humanlike animals. He explained that by moving tissue from one creature to another or by moving it around on an animal, it is possible to graft tissue into humanlike shapes and alter its future growth. This claim may or may not be true. Moreau's beasts were by no means perfect. They had awkward gaits and ungainly proportions. Many had useless limbs, hunchbacks, and unnatural hair growth. They all had deformed faces and unusually shaped hands. Nevertheless, there is no doubt that Dr. Moreau's knowledge of surgical alteration techniques was well beyond his time.[5]

Uncomfortable in His Own Skin?

Moreau's interest in reshaping animals may have originally stemmed from a subconscious desire to compensate for his own physical problems. The doctor suffered from an unidentified skin condition that required him to restrict sun exposure. In one film version of Dr. Moreau's life, he wears wide hats, sunglasses with extra side shades, and hoods, as well as a thick white sunscreen powder. As a result, Dr. Moreau looks hideously pale and may have been self-conscious about his appearance.

Psychopathology: Narcissism

Above and beyond the symptoms of a delusional disorder, which can be temporary, Dr. Moreau demonstrates many of the symptoms of narcissistic personality disorder, which is often an intractable problem. Individuals with this condition are extraordinarily self-absorbed and self-centered, to the point that they

---

5. Dr. Seth Brundlefly would not combine human and animal DNA via teleportation for another hundred years.

lack empathy for others and have grandiose beliefs about themselves.

Can't be bothered to explain his research. When an outsider ends up on Moreau's island, he denies the man any explanation of his research. Furthermore, despite the rapid advances and contribution to the field of biology, Dr. Moreau feels no need to share his accomplishments with the rest of the scientific community. Indeed, he seems to have no desire for recognition from his peers. This is likely due to Dr. Moreau's narcissistic beliefs that his brilliance is unique and could be understood only by a select few.

Requires excessive admiration. Moreau uses some of the creatures he has made as his personal servants and pets. When they survive but fail to achieve the perfect balance between man and animal that Moreau is striving for, their sole purpose seems to be to wait on him and admire him. Instead of regarding Moreau as an equal, many of these servile creatures seem to regard him as their father or as some sort of god incarnate. A number of the more human hybrids actively worship Dr. Moreau, chanting praises about his greatness and power.

Grandiose sense of self-importance. Although Moreau could have simply abandoned the line of research that his university objected to, he instead thought himself so important that he deserved to continue his work regardless of what the law or academia said. This is a classic example of how narcissism can lead to illegal and criminal behaviors in the mad scientist: Moreau believes his talents are so phenomenal that he thinks he should be above the law and exempt from the morality that guides the rest of civilization.

Repeated torture of other humans and animals. Though harming others is also a symptom of antisocial personality disorder, in Dr. Moreau's case this behavior is probably prompted by his lack of empathy for others, also a symptom of narcissistic personality disorder. Moreau simply does not recognize the feelings of others, even as they lie writhing in pain on the vivisection table. His idealistic vision of "humanizing" these animals as a favor to them overrides all the telltale signs of torture and exploitation. On the brighter side, Dr. Moreau does not seem to take sadistic pleasure in torturing other creatures, as have some other mad scientists.[6]

Physical and moral self-isolation. In addition to these narcissistic qualities, Dr. Moreau has effectively isolated himself from the input of other scientists (and in fact, from most other humans). After being banned from England, Moreau fenced himself off on an island for more than ten years. Isolation from human contact can exacerbate psychological problems. The result of years spent alone or in the company of genetically mutated animal offspring is demonstrated when Moreau chooses not to bother dealing with his sole visitor's panic about the grotesque animals he has seen—Moreau considers it a waste of his time. Moreau has clearly lost perspective on how far from the norm he has strayed. Even on an abandoned island, Moreau prefers to be alone for most of his days, working on his creatures in a gore-stained operating room.

Conclusion

Dr. Moreau used his knowledge of vivisection to play God, creating beastly patchwork animal-humans who worshipped him as some

6. The CIA chemist Sidney Gottlieb enjoyed poisoning other people with psychoactive drugs, including his friends, coworkers, and homeless people he met randomly on the street.

sort of deity. The doctor's narcissistic traits prompted him to continue his work in isolation, avoiding further critique of his unorthodox methods while taking mad science to a new level of creepiness. In the end, Dr. Moreau suffers death at the paws of his last creation, a semi-human puma who escapes from her shackles and exacts animal revenge on the evil man who caused her pain.

Diagnosis

Axis I: Delusional disorder, grandiose type
Axis II: Narcissistic personality disorder
Axis III: Unidentified dermatological condition
Axis IV: Dangerous home environment due to presence of possibly violent creatures
Axis V: GAF = 55—moderate difficulty: few human friends; conflicts with peers; social isolation

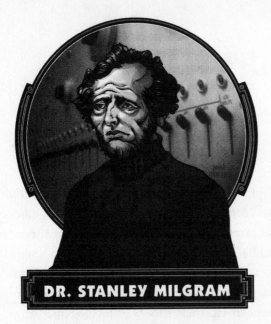

DR. STANLEY MILGRAM

(1933–1984)

"Relatively few [of my research] subjects experienced greater tension than a nail-biting patron at a good Hitchcock thriller."
—Dr. Stanley Milgram

Birthplace: The Bronx, New York, U.S.A.

Primary goal: To find out what makes humans tick

Political party affiliation: Republican

Likes: Playing darts while high on peyote; shocking people

Lesser known fact: Invented the concept of "six degrees of separation"

Reported IQ: 158 (extremely high)

Hobby: Tricking people into believing that he had psychic abilities

Genius:

Madness:

Introduction

Stanley Milgram was a founding father of social psychology whose experiments centered on the principles of obedience. By all accounts an extremely intelligent man, Milgram's voracious curiosity seems to have outweighed any squeamishness about taking psychological experiments to the utmost limits of human experience. In experiments on innocent civilians and in research on himself, Milgram applied electrical shock, hallucinogenic drugs, and what many today consider mental torture. Though his experimental practices strayed far from tasteful norms, and though many considered Milgram himself to be an arrogant experimenter constantly willing to play God, his research laid the cornerstone of social psychology and exposed the evil undercurrent that pulses just beneath the surface of even the most normal people (yes, that includes your sweet mother).

Portrait of a Social Scientist

Milgram's teachers first noticed his high intelligence when he was in kindergarten, but it wasn't until he took an intelligence test in high school that he was placed in advanced classes. With a reported intelligence quotient (IQ) of 158, Milgram's intellect was rated in the "extremely high" range. The average IQ is 100, and 68 percent of the population's IQ scores fall between 85 and 115.

Another 14 percent receive scores in the 116–130 range, and only 2 percent score between 131 and 145. Out of about 300 million people in the United States, only about 40,000 score above 145. In other words, Milgram was smarter than the vast majority of Americans.

Wielding a top-rate brain, Milgram had no trouble navigating the halls of academia at Queens College, where he studied political science, and at Harvard University, where he received his Ph.D. in Social Psychology in 1960 at the age of twenty-seven. Milgram's first job was as an assistant professor at Yale. After three years, he returned to Harvard to work as a professor. He was never granted tenure at Harvard, which many believe was due to negative publicity surrounding the unorthodox and arguably unethical experimental methods that were the hallmark of his academic career.

There were a number of incidents in Milgram's childhood that foreshadowed the type of scientist he would become. First, it should be noted that having a high IQ does not guarantee that a child won't do stupid things. In Milgram's case, during his childhood he and some friends combined volatile chemicals from a chemistry set and lowered them over the edge of a bridge into a river. The resulting explosion was large enough to warrant someone calling the fire department. In addition to getting in trouble with his friends, Milgram and his brother often worked together to engage in deceptive behaviors. In one incident, the Milgram boys created an elaborate scheme in which they successfully used trickery and lies to convince a friend that Milgram had psychic abilities. This friend may have been Milgram's first research *subject* (a term used in research to describe people who are being studied or participating in an experiment). Even as a child, Stanley Milgram was carefully designing and conducting experiments that involved the deception and control of others.

Uncovering Shocking Evil

Milgram's most famous research question was simple: How much pain will a person inflict on another human being if someone in authority tells them to? A number of previous experiments had demonstrated that people are likely to conform to group beliefs, including changing their answer about the length of a line to agree with everyone else, even if the group is blatantly wrong. But Milgram was not satisfied with these results; he wanted to investigate people's responses to authority when something much more important than the length of a line was in question. Drawing on deep creativity and a strong understanding of experimental design, Milgram concocted an experiment that elegantly answered this question, though it required deception and may have inflicted mental trauma.

Milgram invited a range of subjects into the laboratory, from Yale college students to middle-aged welders and prim elderly ladies. Subjects were told that they were participating in a study about the effects of punishment on learning. Each subject began the experiment with another subject, who was actually a *confederate*—a member of the research team. The subject and the confederate drew pieces of paper to determine the "teacher" and the "learner" in the experiment. Both pieces of paper said "teacher," so that the subject would always be assigned to the role of teacher. An official experimenter in a laboratory coat explained that the learner would be learning a list of words, and would be given a mild shock each time he got a word incorrect. The subject watched as the learner was taken into an adjacent room, strapped into a chair, and electrodes placed on his arms. Milgram's attention to detail was hilariously frightening, as at this point the strapped-in confederate casually mentioned that he had a heart condition. The subject was then taken into a room and shown an elaborate machine with wires coming out of the back; it read "SHOCK GENERATOR, TYPE ZLB, DYSON INSTRUMENT COMPANY, WALTHAM, MASS. OUTPUT 15 VOLTS—450 VOLTS." Thirty switches were placed in increasing shock order across the machine's front panel, with labels ranging from "SLIGHT SHOCK" all the way up to "SEVERE SHOCK," and on the highest levels simply the foreboding label, "XXX."

Built on a solid foundation of deception, the mental torture portion of the experiment was set to begin. The subject was instructed to begin with switch one and to give an increasing shock level each time the learner made a mistake. And the poor confederate learner made a lot of mistakes. Each subsequent mistake and increasing shock level elicited cries of pain from the learner[1]. If the subject hesitated to deliver the next shock level, the lab coat–wearing experimenter followed a scripted set of authoritative and calm prompts, such as "please continue" and "if the learner doesn't answer in a reasonable time, consider it wrong and follow the same procedure you have been doing for a wrong answer."

Ultimately, variations on these experimental procedures were conducted with hundreds of subjects. The results showed that humans demonstrate a striking obedience to authority in inflicting pain on others. In the first set of experiments, 65 percent of subjects went all the way up to the "450 VOLTS/XXX" shock level, despite hearing hysterical screams followed by dead silence from the learner, who had failed to learn the words and apparently paid dearly for it. Some subjects were more nervous or upset about the process than others, but the majority obeyed. After reaching the highest level of shock they could inflict, subjects were let in on the ruse and were told that the learner was not actually shocked. (Sort of like an ultra-sadistic *Candid Camera* or *Punk'd*, but with

1. To ensure that the subjects in every experiment had the same experience, these panicked whimpers and shouts of unfathomable agony were actually recordings.

less laughing and more mental torture.) After years of conducting these experiments, the thorough-minded Milgram concluded that the majority of people, regardless of their *demographic characteristics* (defined as stable features such as gender, age, socioeconomic status) will comply with commands as long as they believe they come from a legitimate authority with an official lab coat. Milgram did not predict the backlash of publicity—people were both outraged at Milgram's methods and horrified by the dark features of human nature he had uncovered.

Substance Use and Creativity

The intellectual skill that set Milgram apart from many of his colleagues was the ability to apply experimental designs to complex social phenomena. This flexibility and creativity was somewhat evident when Milgram was a child but seemed to increase as he matured. This mental flexibility may have been due to the stimulating academic environments that Milgram chose to immerse himself in, or it may have been the stimulating array of substances Milgram chose to smoke, snort, and sniff. The 1950s and 1960s were a wild time to be a scientist—it was commonly theorized that hallucinogenic drugs led to expanded awareness and increased creativity. This was in part based on reports by hallucinogen users that the drugs induced *synesthesia*, a cross-sensory experience in which stimulation of one sensory system leads to perception in another, such as hearing a song and seeing visions that correspond to the sounds of the music. Milgram was eager to explore this new avenue of creativity.

While a graduate student at Harvard, Milgram and some fellow students took peyote, a cactus containing mescaline—and one of the oldest known hallucinogenic drugs. In addition to synesthesia, mescaline can produce vivid mental images and distorted vision, other heightened sensory experiences, and altered perceptions of

space and time. In addition to peyote, Milgram reportedly occasionally used marijuana, psychedelic mushrooms, cocaine, and
amphetamines. Although no research has conclusively demonstrated
that drug use increases creativity, Milgram's ability to design very
clever experimental methods for plumbing the depths of the human
mind may have stemmed from his drug-fueled exploration of his
own. On the other hand, many of the effects of hallucinogenic
drugs are due to the user's *expectations,* or what they think they
will experience.[2] Milgram's increased creativity may have occurred
because, like many scientists at the time, that is what Milgram
expected would happen.

Psychopathology:
Narcissism or Justified Self-Confidence?

Judge him how you like, but nobody can say that Stanley Milgram
didn't have a mad scientist's balls of steel and abundance of self-
confidence. In 1954, he applied to the graduate program at Harvard to study social psychology, despite having never taken a
psychology course in his life. The department refused to admit him,
pointing out that Milgram knew nothing about sociology or psychology. In response, Milgram appealed personally to the department chair and secretly enrolled in six social science courses in a
single summer from three different colleges. This persistence paid
off and the department admitted him on a trial basis. Milgram certainly believed in himself, and this self-confidence helped him get
what he wanted on numerous occasions.

But for some things, no amount of self-confidence will help. In
1960, Milgram asked the government for financing to fund his

---

2. For further explanation of expectancy effects, see Dr. Jekyll,
pp. 139–47.

peyote research. He proposed having subjects ingest the substance before undergoing a number of cognitive and physical tests regarding their aesthetic perceptions of art. The U.S. government was not excited about spending money on consciousness-expanding drug research. So what led Milgram to think that he might have a chance of obtaining this sort of funding?

One could argue that this sort of behavior stems from an inflated sense of self-worth and self-importance, one of the symptoms of narcissistic personality disorder Individuals with narcissistic personalities often have a sense of entitlement and expect especially favorable treatment. Milgram may have expected to be awarded funding for his peyote research simply because he viewed himself as "special." Milgram's response to being denied funding was to smoke peyote with some friends and then perform controlled experiments on their abilities to play darts. Data collected from the infamous dart game was colated and catalogued for publication, without government funding. Regardless of what his scientific justification was for studying a bar game while under the influence, we again see Milgram's persistence and creativity at play. Although he demonstrated a sense of self-importance at times, it seems to have been largely justified. What Stanley Milgram was not able to accomplish with intelligence and creativity, he accomplished with persistence and stubborn self-confidence.

Shockingly Sadistic?

To the untrained eye, shocking other people (even in a strictly controlled experiment) may seem like *sadistic* behavior—the derivation of pleasure from inflicting pain. However, the only psychological diagnosis that involves sadism is in the category of sexual and gender identity disorders. For example, a diagnosis of *sexual sadism* is made when an individual finds the psychological or physical suffering of a victim to be sexually exciting and has acted on these urges with a nonconsenting person. There is no evidence that Stanley Milgram was excited by shocking other people, sexually or otherwise. On the other hand, one might argue that by continuing his shock experiments Milgram showed a reckless disregard for the safety of others, a symptom of antisocial personality disorder. Even so, Milgram's disregard was not for people's physical safety, as the experimental setup was not physically dangerous. If anything, he may have disregarded the possible psychological distress that people who participated in his studies might experience.

Milgram's experiments occurred before proper safeguards were in place for the study of human subjects, and he eventually came to realize this. Milgram often referred to the fact that most subjects were happy to have participated in a study that helped us better understand human obedience to authority. However, he also made a personal decision to not complete any further studies in which subjects were tricked, stating, "It is not nice to lure people into the laboratory and ensnare them into a situation that is stressful and unpleasant." Although he stopped these experiments, Milgram was continuously involved in a debate about how human experimental participants should be treated. Milgram coined the term *debriefing*, which refers to the process of informing participants that they have been duped after the experiment is over, and allowing them to react in the presence of the experimenter to make sure they are not experiencing undue distress after the procedures.

Conclusion

Milgram's work prompted a debate in the field of psychology about the ethics of using deception in experimental settings. Researchers who wish to use deception now must provide a convincing argument that the ends justify the means—the benefit of the knowledge that will be gained by tricking individuals must outweigh the personal physical or psychological risks. Additionally, Milgram's use of debriefing served as a prototype for all psychologists, and subsequently ethics boards began requiring debriefing in studies where subjects were deceived. All proposed experiments that study humans now have a section titled "Protection of Human Subjects." In a roundabout way, Milgram's experiments ultimately made us all a little safer from the probing experiments of new generations of mad scientists.

Diagnosis

Axis I: History of hallucinogen intoxication
Axis II: No diagnosis
Axis III: No diagnosis
Axis IV: Experienced high levels of media attention
Axis V: GAF = 85–minimal symptoms: transient substance use; mild anxiety; occasional arguments with public

VICTOR FRANKENSTEIN

(First appeared in Mary Shelley's novel *Frankenstein*, 1831)

"You will hear of powers and occurrences such as you have been accustomed to believe impossible."
—Dr. Victor Frankenstein

Nationality: Swiss by birth
Primary goals: Creation of life; destruction of newly created life
Likes: Electricity; hunchbacks
Dislikes: Playing God and being called on it
Nickname: The modern Prometheus

Genius:

Madness:

Introduction

A mainstay of the big screen and written page, Victor Frankenstein is a classic prototype for all mad scientists. While his initial intentions are not evil, he gets carried away in his quest for knowledge about the fundamentals of life itself. Ultimately, Victor Frankenstein wields the godlike power of being able to give life to inanimate flesh. He is unable to resist using it to create a humanlike creature, just to see if he can do it. Overwhelmed by workaholic tendencies, Frankenstein's laboratory work eventually brings doom to his entire family. The mad scientist is surprisingly emotional and struggled with depression and mania. Who knew that when Frankenstein wasn't shouting "It's alive!" into the heavens, he actually had a very sensitive side?

Portrait of a Scientist

Victor was born in Geneva, Switzerland, and was the eldest child of a government official and his wife. Victor described his father as being kind and dedicated to his children's education. Victor learned Latin and English as a boy, as well as drawing and literature. Victor had a best friend during his childhood and fondly recalls putting on Robin Hood plays with him. Unfortunately, tragedy struck the Frankenstein family and Victor's mother passed away from scarlet fever when he was only seventeen.[1]

There is significant evidence that Victor is extremely intelligent, particularly in the area of verbal intellectual skills. As a child, he reportedly enjoyed reading books and dramas, and was described as curious and bright. He chose to read complex books that were well

1. Mad mathematician Oliver Heaviside also suffered from scarlet fever, a common malady of the preindustrial age.

above his age level. As an adult, Victor was eloquent and wise, adjectives that are frequently used to describe individuals with high levels of verbal intelligence. Medical doctors often have highly developed verbal reasoning skills, which contribute to doctors' abilities to make complex diagnostic judgments that require verbal categorization.

After being educated at home by his father, Victor began to show an interest in philosophy. One of the texts that Victor read was by Cornelius Agrippa, on occult philosophy. This text included chapters on topics such as reviving of the dead, the forming of man, attracting celestial gifts, and how the passions of the mind can work on another's body. Despite his father's statement that Agrippa's work was "sad trash," Victor was fascinated by the subjects of magic, philosophy, and the human form.[2] He began searching for the elixir of life and dreamed of bringing ghosts and devils to life with electricity.

As a young man, Victor attended the University of Ingolstadt, where he studied natural philosophy. This was essentially the study of chemistry and medicine. Victor was especially intrigued by one of his professors, who claimed that scientists could work magic and inspired him to study all areas of science.

Scientific Accomplishments: Mad Biology

Victor Frankenstein began studying what made the human body decay and what made it live. Like other mad scientists, Victor was easily absorbed in his work and there is evidence that he was a workaholic.[3] Though not a diagnostic term, excessive involvement in work activities can cause clinically significant distress and inter-

2. Noted mad rocket scientist Jack Parsons developed a similarly strong belief in the power of the occult.
3. Marie Curie might also have been considered a workaholic.

personal problems. When workaholic tendencies cause substantial problems, they are typically considered to be diagnosable as an occupational problem, or, if excessive working is causing problems in relationships, as a relational problem. In any case, Victor worked for days and nights without stopping, driven by a desire to uncover the secrets of life and death. Victor reported that he spent days at a time in graveyards and burial sites beneath churches, observing the process of death and decay. Through it all, Dr. Frankenstein never lost sight of his goal to reanimate dead tissue.

Not thinking of the larger ramifications of his actions, Dr. Frankenstein spent months collecting the body parts necessary to reanimate a humanlike creature. He reported that he had not initially intended for his creature to be large, but found it easier to work with big chunks of flesh. Thus, his creature ended up being eight feet tall and was made of body parts that Frankenstein collected from graves, dissecting rooms, and his local slaughterhouse and then transported to his attic laboratory.

There is some evidence that Frankenstein's work was driven by symptoms of mania, which include elevated mood, drive, and productivity. Frankenstein describes himself as having a "frantic impulse" to continue his work and became completely absorbed in this sole pursuit, to the point that he stopped corresponding with his family. Ironically, as Dr. Frankenstein toiled to create life, his own health deteriorated and he reportedly became physically emaciated from overworking.

Frankenstein's monster has often been misnamed as "Frankenstein" but in Shelley's book it is referred to as his creature, demon, fiend, devil, and wretch. There is no doubt that what Dr. Frankenstein was able to accomplish in his creation of the monster was unnatural, and in fact he calls his own creation a "vile insect." But he also describes his work with pride, fawning over the creature's "lustrous black and flowing" hair and his "pearly white" teeth. This marveling ends the second the monster comes to life and Dr. Frankenstein is confronted with the real product of his scientific research.[4]

Reanimation Reality: Horror and Hallucinations

It was not until after the creature came to life that Dr. Frankenstein had a "breathless horror and disgust" fill his heart. When the monster reaches out to him, Dr. Frankenstein fears for his life and makes a run for it. In the face of this traumatic event, he uses avoidant coping strategies to keep himself from having to confront the monster he has created. *Coping strategies* are things that people think or do in order to minimize, tolerate, or endure fearful events. Avoidant coping strategies are related to adjustment problems following stressful events and include approaches such as using distractions to try not to think about a problem. For an entire day, Victor Frankenstein simply does not go to his upstairs laboratory, which contains the shambling hulk of a reanimated patchwork corpse. When an old friend comes to town and comments that Victor looks ill, he avoids talking about what has happened.

When the creature escapes, Victor is even somewhat relieved, thinking that he can finally get some needed rest. Soon after, however, Victor experiences symptoms of psychosis, including hallucinations that the monster is attacking him.[5] Concerned, his visiting friend confines Dr. Frankenstein to bed rest where he stays, ranting about monsters, for months: Even after he is largely recovered, Frankenstein reports that the sight and smell of chemicals was star-

---

4. Mad scientists are not always delighted with what they create. Dr. Henry Jekyll was also horrified by the result of his most advanced experimental research.

5. For a more detailed explanation of post-traumatic stress disorder, see p. 53.

tling to him, but he is able to return to full functioning and to his studies within a year. Sadly, Victor's horrors were only beginning. After having largely forgotten about the creature, Victor received a letter indicating that his younger brother had been murdered. When he returns home to be with his family, Victor finds his creature lurking near his hometown and it becomes clear that the monster has murdered his brother. A family friend is tried and executed for the crime, so Victor bears the further horror of knowing that his creation killed his brother and an innocent person paid for the crime.

Ultimately, Dr. Frankenstein meets his monster in the mountains, and the creature, rejected by all whom it has met, asks for the doctor's care. In an affirmation of Dr. Frankenstein's biology skills, the creature turns out to be sentient, articulate, intelligent, and has taught itself language. But like his creator, Frankenstein's monster is brought to misery by the knowledge it has gained. Realizing that it is a monstrosity and not really human, Frankenstein's monster wishes that it had not even learned to speak. The creature convinces the good doctor to create it a mate, swearing that it will leave all humans in peace if it can only have someone to love. When Dr. Frankenstein takes too long, the fiend systematically kills the doctor's best friend and then his wife.

Psychopathology: Melancholia

After Victor Frankenstein endured the loss of so many family members, he began traveling the world in search of the monster. It was during this lonely mission that he began to develop symptoms of major depressive disorder. In Frankenstein's day, physical and mental illnesses were still sometimes defined by imbalances in the *humors,* which were naturally occurring body fluids. Blood, yellow bile, phlegm, and black bile were thought to lead to physiological and mental health when properly balanced, but when an excess of black bile occurred, it could lead to melancholic moods. A nineteenth-century doctor might have diagnosed Frankenstein with an imbalance in his humors, in particular an overabundance of black bile. In fact, many of the features of melancholy would today be considered symptoms of depression:

Fitful sleep. The doctor is described as sleeping poorly and gnashing his teeth. In fact, sleep disturbances are a frequently occurring symptom of depression. Insomnia is the most common sleep disturbance experienced by depressed individuals, with 80 percent reporting difficulty falling asleep or staying asleep. It may be that sleep disturbances promote mood problems, as not getting enough sleep can disrupt such mood-balancing brain chemicals as serotonin and dopamine. In Victor Frankenstein's case, his inability to sleep well may have been prompted by "guilt and woe" and over time led to an increase in symptoms of depressed mood.

Low or depressed mood. Dr. Frankenstein is described as being "destroyed by misery" and "overcome by gloom." Depressed mood can be self-reported (a subjective experience reported by an individual) or it can be observed by others in an individual's behaviors, such as appearing tearful or sad. In fact, Frankenstein reports feeling down and also appears gloomy and miserable to others for more than a two-week period, thus meeting one of the main symptom criteria for major depressive disorder.

Feelings of worthlessness or excessive guilt. It is difficult to assess whether Victor Frankenstein's feelings of guilt over creating his monster are excessive or appropriate given his actions. Regardless, Victor reports excessive guilt and consequently withdraws into solitude. Feelings of guilt are understandable, given that Victor's science experiment has gone aggro and murdered everyone he loves.

Major loss. Like his fellow mad scientist Marie Curie, Victor Frankenstein's depressive symptoms were precipitated by a major loss in his life. Research indicates that the majority of depressive episodes follow a loss or major life transition, such as a loss of a romantic relationship, friendship, job, or a move. In Dr. Frankenstein's case, he reported that he had lost "everything" and could not "begin life anew." In addition to the loss of his mother during adolescence, Frankenstein was likely referring to the loss of his friend, the innocent noble human he had created, and the subsequent loss of all of his meaningful relationships.

Conclusion

Victor Frankenstein was a workaholic with a tendency to isolate himself from others. His scientific endeavors were spurred by the desire to understand the fundamentals of life and death, and Frankenstein's thirst for knowledge (and a little mania) fueled him to do what should have been scientifically impossible: breathe life into a collection of spare human parts. In a prelude to worse things to come, Victor showed alarming signs of psychosis stemming from the traumatic experience of giving life to an undead creature.[6] After experiencing the horrible fallout of his actions, Dr. Frankenstein plummeted into a major depressive episode before being murdered by his own monster in the Arctic.

6. This severely emotional reaction may be due to Dr. Frankenstein's sensitive nature, as other mad doctors have performed similar feats without the angst (see Dr. Moreau, pp. 81–88).

Diagnosis

Axis I: Major depressive disorder, Severe, Recurrent; Psychotic disorder not otherwise specified (hallucinations); Bereavement

Axis II: No diagnosis

Axis III: History of malnutrition

Axis IV: Lives in harsh environmental conditions (the Arctic)

Axis V: GAF = 30–very serious impairment: suicidal ideation; major depression; insomnia

SIDNEY GOTTLIEB

(1918–1999)

*"This [top secret] project will include . . . a study of the
biochemical, neurophysiological, sociological, and
clinical psychiatric aspects of L.S.D."*
—Dr. Sidney Gottlieb

Birthplace: The Bronx, New York, U.S.A.

Primary goals: Overthrow Fidel Castro by any means
necessary; become a master of mind control

Likes: Toxin-soaked Cuban cigars; sampling his own
hallucinogenic concoctions

Dislikes: Boring parties

Nicknames: The Prime Poisoner; America's Real-Life Q; Dr.
Strangelove

Alias: Joseph Scheider

Favorite project: MK-ULTRA, a secret CIA program
  investigating mind control
Lesser known fact: Gave Timothy Leary his first hit of LSD
Awards: Distinguished Intelligence Medal

Genius:

Madness:

Introduction

Sidney Gottlieb worked for the Central Intelligence Agency
(CIA) during the height of the Cold War between the United
States and Russia. As head of the chemical division in the CIA's
technical services, Gottlieb personally oversaw years of reckless
experimentation with newly discovered hallucinogenic substances.
With these newfound psychotropic drugs and a looming Russian
threat, Gottlieb seems to have felt it was his duty to inflict his
nauseous experiments on anyone and everyone, including innocent civilians. During his career, Gottlieb invented hundreds of
assassination techniques, most aimed at eliminating the surprisingly hardy Fidel Castro[1] and other world leaders. A talented
chemist with few moral reservations, Sidney Gottlieb wanted
nothing less than to perfect a system of mind control in time to
beat the Rooskies.

---

1. Fidel was still alive when this book went to press and is presumably
safe from assassination attempts now that Gottlieb has passed on.

Portrait of a Scientist

Sidney Gottlieb was born in the Bronx in 1918 to Orthodox Jewish parents who had immigrated from Hungary. The young Sidney had a stutter (which persisted into adulthood) and was also born with a club foot (which affected his gait as an adult). Alfred Adler, one of the fathers of child psychology, theorized that children often engage in overcompensation to make up for physical impairments such as these. Adler called this the *inferiority complex*. In fact, Sidney did exhibit symptoms of an underlying inferiority complex: To compensate for his speech impairment, he got a Master's degree in Speech Therapy; and to compensate for his physical disabilities, Sidney religiously practiced folk dancing.

Sidney went to the University of Wisconsin for college and received his Ph.D. in Chemistry from the California Institute of Technology in 1943, specializing in psychoactive and toxic chemicals. While at Cal Tech in the 1940s, Sidney met and married his wife. Though Dr. Gottlieb may have been downright evil in his professional life, there is no evidence that he had any difficulties in his private family life. He and his wife lived happily together and had four children. Nothing is known about what Dr. Gottlieb did between 1943 and 1951, when he joined the CIA. Many people believe he was involved in top-secret prisoner interrogations for the U.S. military during World War II.

Morally Questionable Achievements

Dr. Gottlieb has been referred to as "America's prime poisoner." Though there is no doubt that his motivations were nefarious, his ideas for assassinations were undeniably ingenious. His knowledge of chemistry made him particularly adept at inventing ways to transport and deliver poisonous substances without reducing their potency. Each of the following ideas generated research and planning, although none were carried out to their full lethal conclusion.

⚡ In 1960, Gottlieb attempted to assassinate Lumumba, the dictator of Zaire. He developed a way of transporting a fatal bacteria that was native to Africa in a substance that could then be injected into Lumumba's toothpaste tube.

⚡ Cubans love cigars, and Fidel Castro was no different. Gottlieb infused a box of Castro's favorite cigars with botulinum toxin, a deadly poison. Luckily for Fidel, no one could figure out how to deliver the box.

⚡ Gottlieb had other ideas for assassinating Castro, including poison pens, a poison wetsuit, and an exploding conch shell.

⚡ Gottlieb also wanted to spray Castro's television studio with LSD so he would look foolish and confused when addressing the Cuban people.

Unethical, Illegal, and Immoral Scientific Methods

There is no doubt that many of the research methods employed by Gottlieb and his colleagues were unethical. Like many scientists at the time, Gottlieb believed that hallucinogens like LSD would have a number of useful applications and even took the drug himself.[2] Gottlieb was interested in studying the effects of these sorts of drugs on individuals' mental states, with the goal of being able to use mind control to the CIA's advantage. At the same time that

2. This is a common trait of mad scientists, sometimes with harmless results (see Dr. Stanley Milgram, Gottlieb's contemporary, pp. 89–98) and other times with shocking and fatal results (see Dr. Henry Jekyll pp. 139–47).

ethics in research involving human subjects was beginning to be important in the public sphere, the CIA operated in a secret sphere and Gottlieb was not held to these principles.

Under operation MK-ULTRA, Gottlieb helped design experiments to test various mind control techniques, including the use of hallucinogens, electroshock therapy, and sensory deprivation. Gottlieb believed that he could figure out how to wipe a man's identity and replace it with a substitute identity, thus creating the perfect spy. He also hoped to develop and test formulas that would lead to easy interrogations of prisoners. These experiments were performed on extremely vulnerable populations, including political detainees in Vietnam during the Vietnam War, imprisoned African American heroin addicts in Kentucky, misinformed prostitutes, and other unsuspecting civilians and CIA operatives.

Operation Midnight Climax. One of Gottlieb's projects involved using CIA safe houses in New York and San Francisco to set up parties in which prostitutes working for the CIA would dose their johns with LSD or other drugs in order to observe the effects that the combination of sex and drugs might have on an unknowing operative or prisoner. These oblivious men were filmed and photographed, as well as interviewed while hallucinating.

Operation MK-PILOT. Gottlieb also oversaw a clearly unethical experiment in which imprisoned drug addicts were offered heroin as a reward for participating in mind control experiments. Not only were these subjects motivated to "consent" because of their addiction, they were taken advantage of specifically because they were imprisoned and could be observed for long periods of time. Some of these individuals were exposed to more than two months straight of LSD dosing, which Gottlieb concluded had few negative effects.

Lack of informed consent. These sorts of experiments clearly demonstrate the ethical importance of obtaining informed consent from research subjects. At least one victim died after being administered a drug. The experiments also demonstrate the strength of dehumanization. In social psychology research, dehumanization refers to the phenomenon by which people are more likely to engage in cruelty and violence toward others if they do not think of the others as complete humans. In the case of many of MK-ULTRA's victims, Gottlieb and those he worked with may have been able to engage in such deplorable behaviors because they did not view drug addicts, prostitutes, or ethnic minorities as fully human.

Psychopathology: Government-Sanctioned Antisocial Personality Disorder

Although many criminals are referred to as *sociopaths* or *psychopaths*, these terms are not actually psychological or psychiatric diagnoses. Instead, researchers generally consider sociopathy and psychopathy as personality defects that lead to criminal and antisocial behavior. According to the current diagnostic criteria, an individual with pervasive sociopathic or psychopathic traits would meet criteria for antisocial personality disorder. Like many other mad scientists, Gottlieb shows some of the symptoms of antisocial personality disorder.[3]

Reckless disregard for the safety of others. Gottlieb repeatedly assaulted unknowing victims by sneaking LSD and other hallucinogens into their drinks, despite knowing that this could have nega-

---

3. Dr. Evil, Trofim Lysenko, and Dr. No all exhibit some degree of these symptoms as well.

tive effects. In one particularly drastic event, Gottlieb spiked the drink of one of the CIA's own operatives, Dr. Frank Olson, with LSD, presumably as some sort of joke, or perhaps as preparation for a potentially similar attack that could come from the Russians. Olson was initially terrified, and in the weeks following being drugged he became unusually depressed, anxious, agitated, and erratic. Soon after, he tragically fell thirteen stories to his death.[4]

Deceitfulness and lying. Ultimately, Gottlieb passed away before he was found guilty of any crime. This was partly because he hid the truth by methodically destroying all CIA records pertaining to his work on MK-ULTRA's mind control experiments, truth serums, and poisons and their delivery systems.

Total lack of remorse. There is minimal evidence that Gottlieb regretted his reckless endangerment of others' well-being. However, he did ultimately conclude in 1972 that hallucinogens were not likely to be helpful in mind control, because their effects varied dramatically from one individual to another.

A fully functional frontal lobe. Gottlieb does not fully meet the criteria for antisocial personality disorder, because he does not exhibit impulsivity and a failure to plan ahead. Instead, his schemes were planned well in advance and executed methodically. In fact, there is some evidence that in the Cold War environment, Gottlieb believed that what he was doing was an essential part of the effort to maintain democracy and fight communism throughout the world. Like Lex Luthor, Gottlieb also had a philanthropic side and demonstrated some empathetic characteristics. When he retired

4. Olson may have suffered from *hallucinogen persisting perception disorder,* in which the perceptual alterations of a hallucinogen persist after the substance has been metabolized.

from the CIA he reportedly volunteered at a leper hospital in India for more than a year.

Conclusion

Sidney Gottlieb was a master of mind-altering chemicals and a master of clandestine operations. There is no denying that he mis-used the scientific method by studying people's reactions to mind control techniques without their consent, and that he showed symptoms of antisocial personality disorder. But Gottlieb was also a husband, father, and philanthropist. Despite the appalling outcome of his research endeavors, Gottlieb thought that taking advantage of unwitting subjects was the American thing to do.

Diagnosis

Axis I: History of hallucinogen intoxication
Axis II: Antisocial personality disorder
Axis III: Club feet (probably cerebral palsy)
Axis IV: No diagnosis
Axis V: GAF = 80–slight impairment: inferiority complex; grossly inappropriate social interactions

Died in the Name of Science

For a mad scientist, there is no difference between work and play. The hours spent in a laboratory, devoid of human contact, are hours spent pursuing a dream. When doing science is synonymous with living life, you can no more stop working than you can stop breathing. Sadly, the human body is often too frail to support years of solid research, especially on the dangerous forefront of science.

This section examines those who sacrificed their lives in the pursuit of scientific fact. These men and women used lab work to deal with personal loss, as a substitute for human relationships, and even to seek the approval of their peers. But whether they were driven to become their own guinea pigs or just unable to step away from toxic experiments, these mad scientists demonstrated that it's all too easy to be literally consumed by the rigors of scientific endeavor.

DR. SETH BRUNDLE

(First appeared in George Langelaan's short story *The Fly*, 1957)

"I'm working on something that will change the world and human life as we know it."
—Dr. Seth Brundle

Nationality: American
Primary goals: Invent (and perfect) a teleportation machine
Secondary goals: Increase his own percentage of human genetic material
Hair: Thick, all-over-body bristles
Likes: Sugar; sticking to the ceiling
Dislikes: Flytraps; horrified reactions of onlookers
Hobbies: Extreme barroom arm-wrestling
Nickname: Brundlefly
Awards: An inch away from a Nobel Prize in Physics

Genius:

Madness:

Introduction

The actor Jeff Goldblum portrays this idealistic scientist in the 1986 movie *The Fly*. Living alone in a vast, empty warehouse, the young inventor works ceaselessly to perfect a teleportation machine that will revolutionize commerce and transportation. With a woefully neglected social life, Dr. Brundle is psychologically unprepared to deal with the emotional highs and lows accompanying a budding relationship with a beautiful female reporter. The stress affects his scientific judgment and the doctor makes a rash decision to become his own guinea pig. When an ensuing experiment in teleportation goes awry, Dr. Brundle is genetically recombined with a common housefly—with horrific (and fatal) consequences.

Portrait of a Scientist

Seth Brundle most likely experienced a lonely childhood filled with study and exploration. It is doubtful that Seth was a very athletic child—he reported feeling motion sickness to the point of vomiting while riding his tricycle. Later in life, Dr. Brundle is inordinately amazed and empowered as he gains an uncanny insectile super-strength. (A stronger man likely would not have felt the need to immediately arm-wrestle truckers upon discovering his newfound strength.) Based on his skill as an adult pianist, it appears that Seth took years of music lessons as a child. Seth probably spent most of his childhood indoors and alone, just as he spent his adulthood.

Research indicates that solitude in childhood can lead to adjustment problems, including behavior problems and anxiety.

Although his exact academic pedigree is unknown, Seth Brundle did receive his doctoral degree, likely in physics or a related field. Through his research, he demonstrated significant expertise in topics such as teleportation, quantum mechanics, genetics, and computer programming. As an adult, Dr. Brundle did not have any affiliation with an academic institution, choosing to work alone in a home laboratory in an industrial neighborhood.[1] He rarely left his laboratory and even bought many identical versions of the same outfit so he would not have to "expend" his mental energy on petty tasks such as choosing clothing.[2]

Scientific Accomplishment: Teleportation

Prior to his transformation into Brundlefly, Dr. Brundle worked in isolation for six years. It is telling that during this time he was able to invent (although not perfect) a teleportation machine. Although he attended scientific conventions, Dr. Brundle did not share his ongoing work with other scientists. He is quoted as saying that he worked best "on my own."

Brundle may have been right, because his work yielded impressive results. His teleportation devices, called telepods, involved a complex interface between lasers and a molecular identification unit. This unit was able to accurately identify the molecular structures of women's stockings, steaks, and baboons. Inanimate objects were effectively teleported, although animate objects were often delivered inside-out. The system also featured voice recognition security, an impressive feature for the 1980s.

1. Like Dr. Moreau and Dr. Evil, Dr. Brundle also had a piano.
2. Brundle claimed he learned this time-saving trick from Albert Einstein.

Dr. Brundle's dedication to his work was unquestionable. The teleportation machine worked by breaking down an object in one place and rebuilding it elsewhere—essentially creating new life. The road to successful teleportation was paved with the death of at least a few baboons. Dr. Brundle initially had trouble teleporting animate objects, and even raw meat. During these developmental stages, the juicy steaks that he teleported turned out chewy and synthetic and the baboons seemed to be teleported inside-out. The poor bloody transported creatures would twitch for a few minutes before expiring. Before Dr. Brundle could teach his teleportation machine to instill the breath of life into a creature, he had to learn to live himself. It was not until Dr. Brundle experienced the love of a woman that he had a flash of insight and suddenly understood how to program his computer to accurately teleport live flesh. Once he grasped this concept, his machines succeeded in teleporting a baboon. Unfortunately, Brundle himself would not enjoy a similarly successful teleportation.

Psychopathology: Pre-Transformation

During his research, Dr. Brundle demonstrated significant psychological problems.

Extreme paranoia and mistrust of others. Dr. Brundle's paranoia permeated every aspect of his personal and scientific life. In particular, Dr. Brundle showed a number of symptoms of *paranoid personality disorder*. One of the major features of this disorder is pervasive distrust and suspiciousness of others, without sufficient basis for holding such suspicions. At a scientific conference, Dr. Brundle did not present his research because he was convinced that other scientists would malevolently copy his ideas. Rather than share his project with other scientists, Brundle outsourced the design of the components of his teleporter and assembled them himself. This approach ensured that no single subcontractor would construct enough of the machine to understand its function. He was also reluctant to confide in people he did trust—another symptom of the disorder—as he feared that others would eavesdrop. When he got a new girlfriend, he was suspicious that she was cheating on him. In a jealous outburst, Dr. Brundle recklessly decided to teleport himself while drunk. A small housefly joined him in the telepod and Dr. Seth Brundle began his first step toward transformation into the creature called Brundlefly.

Social detachment and flat affect. In addition to paranoia, Dr. Brundle showed some symptoms of isolation and detachment from social relationships, symptoms of *schizoid personality disorder*—not to be confused with schizophrenia. Individuals with schizoid personality disorder do not enjoy or desire close relationships; they almost always choose solitary activities. This certainly describes Dr. Brundle, who bought his own espresso machine so that he did not have to leave his home laboratory and interact with chatty baristas. Individuals with this disorder generally have emotional detachment, flat affect (minimal expression of emotions), and take pleasure in few social activities. Dr. Brundle takes pleasure in his work and shows excitement and other emotions at appropriate times of scientific achievement, as well as sadness and regret when a failed experiment grotesquely kills a baboon.

High functioning scientist, low functioning insect-monster. Prior to his transformation, Dr. Seth Brundle had a number of symptoms of serious psychopathology but was largely able to function adequately in his role as a scientist. Despite isolating himself and worrying that others were out to get him, Brundle managed to pursue a consensual adult romantic relationship. Clearly, his symptoms did not completely impair his social life. Unfortunately, these same symptoms of paranoia and isolation continued after Dr. Brundle's DNA was combined with that of a fly. Combined with what was to come, Brundle faced insurmountable obstacles to enjoying a regular life.

Psychopathology: Post-Transformation

Immediately following his fateful and fatal error, Seth Brundle reportedly felt "like a million bucks." It is likely that the gradual integration of fly DNA into his human genetic material caused Brundle to experience symptoms of mania.[3]

Manic episodes. During this early transformation time period, Brundle demonstrated symptoms of abnormally elevated mood and grandiosity. He declares that his genetic code has been purified and he has been fundamentally improved as a human being. He states that teleportation has "purged" him and made him a "king among men." In his exuberance, Brundle tries to convince his girlfriend to teleport herself, telling her to "drink deep and dive into the plasma pool." These statements clearly indicate an abnormally elevated sense of self-esteem and positive mood. During a breakfast with his girlfriend, Brundle also spoke rapidly and at great length, another symptom of a manic episode.

Although humans (with normal homo sapien DNA) also show symptoms of excessive energy during manic episodes, Brundlefly's human-fly combo DNA exacerbate his symptoms. Brundlefly is extraordinarily energetic in all domains: he makes love to his girlfriend for four hours, develops superhuman flexibility and strength, and gains the reflexes to catch a fly with lightning speed. Brundle-

3. Lex Luthor and Dr. Jekyll also suffered from episodes of mania.

fly soon engages in casual sex, drinking, and gorges himself on candy and sugar.[4] This excessive involvement in pleasurable activities is yet another symptom of mania.

Social consequences of mania compounded with genetic abnormality. Some of the symptoms of mania might sound like fun, but these episodes can have horrible consequences. Individuals in the midst of a manic episode feel compelled to engage in pleasurable activities—often without regard for the possible negative outcomes of their behaviors. In Brundle's case, his elevated mood leads to extreme irritability when his girlfriend refuses to be teleported and he childishly kicks her out of his laboratory. Immediately after ridding himself of his "low" energy girlfriend, he impulsively recruits another woman to teleport. At a local bar, the usually shy Brundle bets a group of men one hundred dollars that he can beat them at arm wrestling. Without human restraint, Brundle breaks a man's arm, ripping the flesh open in a compound fracture. Without demonstrating remorse, Brundle leaves the bar with the man's girlfriend. At home, he assaults her in an attempt to force her to teleport. All of these behaviors during the early transformation phase are consistent with a human-fly hybrid manic episode.

Final Transformation and Decompensation

Brundle's initial exhilaration at being teleported ends quickly when he realizes what he is becoming. He develops strange sores on his face and begins losing his fingernails and teeth. After querying his computer system and finding that he now lives with housefly DNA, he calls himself Brundlefly. He returns to his reclusive ways, insist-

4. Similar episodes of assault, lechery, and drinking are exhibited by Dr. Henry Jekyll after his "purifying" transformation into Mr. Edward Hyde.

ing that he does not want anyone to see him. While his human parts fall off, including his ear, Brundlefly's fly skills continue to increase. Brundlefly can now climb on walls and on the ceiling and subsist on nothing but the sugar in candy. He vomits constantly, only to discover that this is how a fly eats—by hoarking corrosive gastric juices on his meals (or human victims) until they are soft enough to drink.

An initial fascination with his new physiology soon gives way to a resigned horror, as Brundlefly's physical state drives him to desperation. He is lumpy, hairy, twitchy, and bloody. He decides to use his teleportation device to fuse himself with a more pure human sample, effectively reducing his fly DNA. Dr. Brundle's former girlfriend is not very excited to combine her genetic material with Brundlefly's. Lacking human restraint, Brundlefly sadistically vomits on her boss's arm and leg, severing them with corrosive liquid, and then uses brute force to shove his unwilling experimental subject into the teleporter. As Brundlefly's final transformation occurs, he is teleported and fused with his own machine, an extremely painful state of affairs. Mercifully, his former girlfriend puts him out of his misery with a handy shotgun blast to the thorax.

Conclusion

A socially isolated childhood created a brilliant inventor in Dr. Seth Brundle. However, the lack of social skills negatively influenced his research and caused the fateful mistake that resulted in Dr. Brundle's eventual horrific transformation and death. Throughout the course of his genetic transformation, Dr. Brundle demonstrates readily identifiable personality disorders that are often experienced by human beings. Had Dr. Brundle remained human, he might have been able to manage his problems. Unfortunately, these personality traits combined with a dangerous knowledge of science and were enough to lead Dr. Seth Brundle to sacrifice his young life for the noble cause of physics.

Diagnosis

Axis I: Manic episode, Severe

Axis II: Paranoid personality disorder; Schizoid personality disorder

Axis III: Unique medical condition: DNA combined with housefly DNA

Axis IV: Filthy living conditions

Axis V: GAF = 5—minimal functioning: persistent danger of hurting self and others; serious suicidal attempts with clear expectation of death

MADAME MARIE CURIE

(1867–1934)

"[I believe that] humanity will draw more good than evil from new discoveries."
—Marie Curie

Nationality: Polish

Primary goal: Complete understanding of radioactive elements

Hair: Frizzy

Number of Nobel Prizes: Two (Physics, 1903; Chemistry, 1911)

Invented: The portable X-ray machine, used on the battlefield in World War I

First person to: coin the term "radioactive"; be awarded two Nobel Prizes

First woman to: be a professor at the Sorbonne

Nickname: Marya, her given name

Genius:

Madness:

Introduction

Furiously devoted to science and driven to succeed, Madame Marie Curie worked in isolation as a student and then with her husband to discover radium. Throughout her life, Marie was on a roller-coaster ride between incredible professional achievement and devastating personal loss. After the tragic death of her husband, she redoubled her scientific efforts to isolate the element radium into its purest form. Eventually, she succumbed to radiation sickness, the "curious malady" that affected scientific pioneers of radioactivity.

Portrait of a Scientist

Marie Curie had a scientific leg up as a child, with a high school math and science teacher for a father and a school principal for a mother. Even so, Marie faced major educational challenges as a young girl born in 1867 in Warsaw, Poland. Fortunately, she and her four siblings benefited from home instruction from their educated parents that supplemented Warsaw's public school system, and she was able to read before she went to kindergarten.

Unfortunately, Marie's mother passed away from tuberculosis when Marie was only ten years old, and when she was a teenager her older sister also died. These early tragedies did not stop Marie from moving forward in her studies. With her father's encouragement, she graduated from high school at the top of her class at age fifteen. Like her father, Marie was drawn to math and science and was hungry for more knowledge than high school could give her. Unfortunately, the social environment at the time was not conducive to higher education for females.

A Woman Fighting for Education

The late 1800s was not an ideal time to be a female who wanted to be a scientist. In fact, it was not a good time to be a female who wanted any sort of education. Marie received a "gold medal" when she graduated from high school, but this meant little to the male-dominated world of academia. At the time, the Sorbonne University in Paris was the only university in all of Europe that accepted female students. In addition to this obstacle, Marie faced a major financial hurdle—moving to Paris and covering tuition and living expenses was extraordinarily expensive by Polish standards. This led Marie and her older sister, Bronya, to strike an unusual deal that would allow them both to attend the Sorbonne.

After graduating from high school, Marie stayed in Poland and worked as a teacher and private tutor while Bronya moved to Paris and attended medical school at the Sorbonne. Living at home, Marie was able to send her sister all of her income to assist with Parisian living expenses and Sorbonne tuition. During this time of working hard to support her sister, Marie reportedly suffered from some symptoms of depression and her father encouraged her to relax in the countryside with her cousins from time to time. In the evenings, Marie studied on her own and was able to attend clandestine university courses in Poland, which were organized by Polish university professors in defiance of Russian control of the education system.

Finally, after six years of working to support her sister's education, Marie moved to Paris and started her own college education at age twenty-four. In turn, Bronya was able to pay for Marie's expenses. In just three years, Marya, who became known as Marie while in Paris, graduated at the top of her class with a Physics degree. This achievement earned her a scholarship to continue study and a year later she received a master's degree in Mathematics. After briefly working for a French industrial company, Marie pursued her doctoral degree in Physics, focusing on the mysterious rays that emitted from uranium. This degree would not be awarded until 1902, though many have argued that her scientific work merited the degree much earlier. She was the first woman in all of Europe to receive a doctoral degree; her thesis defense committee members pronounced her work to be the greatest scientific contribution ever achieved in a doctoral dissertation.

Radioactivity and Romance

Science permeated Marie's personal life, as well. Marie married her husband Pierre, a physics professor, in 1895. Through Pierre, Marie had access to the resources of academia and laboratory space. The two were inseparable and spent the majority of their time together in their small, cold laboratory.[1] Rumor has it that friends tried to convince the couple to spend more time at home, but Marie and her husband were committed to their work. They even talked about work at the dinner table—when they remembered to stop experimenting and eat. Marie kept detailed, laboratory-like journals of her two daughters' behaviors and physical accomplishments as they grew. Marie was dedicated to her children's education and thought it was important to provide them with learning opportunities outside of school. After the birth of each child, Marie returned to her laboratory within a month.

1. A visiting German professor described the laboratory as "a cross between a stable and a potato cellar."

Ultimately, it was Marie's scientific interests that guided Pierre's work; he abandoned his own research on magnetism to help her investigate the mysterious X-rays scientists had observed.[2] By coining the term *radioactive,* Marie Curie helped identify an entirely novel area of study in chemistry and physics. In 1906, just nine years after marrying, Marie lost her husband and partner in science in a horrific accident. Pierre was likely already suffering from bone cancer due to excessive radiation exposure, which may have contributed to weakness or imbalance. While walking home from the laboratory, he was hurrying to cross a road and was run over by a six-ton horse-drawn wagon. A wheel of the wagon crushed his skull, killing him instantly.

Psychopathology: Depression

While Marie likely suffered from at least one episode of major depression, she also demonstrated resilience in the face of stress.

Major loss precedes depression. Experiencing a major loss in life is one of the most common precursors to a major depressive episode. Marie Curie experienced the loss of her older sister, her mother, and the loss of her husband. Following her husband's death, Marie had significant difficulty returning to work in their laboratory, as Pierre's notes and experiments were everywhere, reminding Marie of her loss. Eventually, she managed to return to work.

Anhedonia. In letters to friends and family, Marie once wrote that even her children could not "awaken life" in her, suggesting she was suffering from anhedonia, one of the major symptoms of depression. *Anhedonia* is diminished interest or pleasure in activities

2. The *X* in X-ray originally stood for "unknown."

or things that were previously interesting or pleasurable. In order to meet criteria for a major depressive episode, an individual must have symptoms of anhedonia or depressed mood that occur for most of the day, almost every day, for a minimum of two weeks. While Marie definitely met these symptom criteria at various points in her life, the diagnosis cannot be made if the loss of a loved one is a possible explanation for the symptoms, which unfortunately for Marie was often the case.

Resilience. The psychological construct of *resilience* refers to an individual's ability to adapt positively when exposed to hazards and risks. Developmental psychologists have investigated early life stressors as risk factors for developing psychological problems. This research uncovered a unique subgroup of children who experienced major early life stressors but emerged "unscathed." If anyone fits the profile of a resilient individual, it is Marie Curie. She experienced major life stressors in a number of domains, including cultural changes, societal expectations, and personal loss, but still lived and worked to the best of her ability.

Fame, Love Affairs, and the Paparazzi

Marie Curie went from relative anonymity and peace to being the focus of intense media, academic, and public scrutiny after she became the first woman to win a Nobel Prize in 1903. Turn-of-the-century paparazzi went so far as to camp outside the Curies' home, hoping to catch a glimpse of the woman who had discovered a new element. Of the constant media attention, Marie wrote, "We are inundated with letters and with visits from photographers and journalists. One would like to dig into the ground somewhere to find a little peace." Coverage of Marie in the French media was favorable until the years after her husband's death.

Just prior to his death, Pierre Curie was offered a position as a professor at the Sorbonne. As part of negotiations for this position, he secured laboratory space for Marie. Despite co-winning a Nobel Prize, Marie was to be relegated to teaching science at a small teacher's college; women simply were not considered to be equipped for the mental rigors of academia. Following Pierre's untimely death, the Sorbonne did something unprecedented; they offered Marie the position that was going to be Pierre's. No woman had held a professorship at the university previously. Both the media and the public felt that given her accomplishments, and given the special circumstances around Pierre's death, this was appropriate.

After acting in this role for four years, Marie nominated herself as a candidate for the physicist seat in the French Academy of Sciences, an all-male national science leadership organization. Also nominated was a Frenchman, Edouard Branly. The media attention directed at Marie suddenly became less favorable. Editorial cartoons printed such captions as "Will a woman get herself into the institute?" Other individuals were upset because Marie was an immigrant and not truly French, and so believed she ought not to be admitted to the Academy. Branly won the seat in the Academy by two votes. As at other times of loss in her life, Marie showed resilience and threw herself back into her work.

The press was unfavorable when the widowed Marie had an affair with a fellow scientist, Paul Langevin (a man with a substantial moustache and a former student of Pierre's). In France at the time, it would have been acceptable for a woman widowed for five years to take a lover, but Langevin was a married man and this was a scandal. While Langevin and Marie attended a conference in Belgium,[3] the media managed to get hold of private letters they had

3. A young Albert Einstein was also present at this conference.

exchanged. Neither could have anticipated the disastrous outcome of the affair. Langevin had been (somewhat unhappily) married, but his wife filed for separation after the letters were published. Anti-Semitic sentiments were present in France and the press accused Marie of being Jewish and a foreigner who had "tarnished the good name" of her deceased French husband and wrecked the home of a decent Frenchwoman. Marie returned to France from the conference in Belgium to find a mob of angry citizens and reporters in front of her home, frightening her young daughters. The Curies hid in a friend's home until the scandal settled down. In the middle of this horrible scandal, Marie Curie was awarded a second Nobel Prize, this one in chemistry, and just for her work in identifying radioactive elements and identifying radioactivity as a core characteristic of the elements. After taking her daughters with her to the award ceremony and publicly thanking their father for his contributions to her work, Marie went into isolation, hiding from the press.

Retreat, Recovery, and Radiation Poisoning

After receiving Nobel Prize number two in 1911, Marie remained secluded for most of 1912. She checked herself into a medical clinic under her maiden name to avoid publicity. She was physically and mentally weak. Physically, she required a kidney operation as her kidney function was weakened by radiation exposure. Mentally, Marie was experiencing what was likely her most severe episode of depression. In addition to the two major symptoms of a major depressive episode (anhedonia and depressed mood), there are seven other symptoms of depression, including change in weight or appetite, insomnia or hypersomnia (inability to sleep or over-sleeping), psychomotor agitation or retardation, fatigue or loss of energy, diminished ability to think or concentrate, recurrent thoughts of death or suicide, and excessive feelings of guilt or worthlessness. Marie felt excessively guilty about her affair with Langevin, to the point that she would no longer allow her daughter Irene to address letters to her as Madame Curie, as she felt unworthy to use his name.

Finally, she returned to France and to her laboratory. In her remaining years of work, Marie worked with her daughter Irene to continue isolating and synthesizing radioactive elements, and worked to establish the Radium Institute. Her depression in full remission, Marie again felt worthy to use her husband's name and in 1914 petitioned to rename the street that the Radium Institute's new building was placed on "Rue Pierre-Curie" in his honor.

World War I had a major impact on lives across Europe and Marie's was no different. Marie and her daughters visited the warfront and were shocked to see the poor conditions of the medical facilities. Marie invented a small X-ray machine that could be transported in a truck onto the battlefield and established 200 permanent X-ray facilities in France and Belgium. These machines were used to detect injuries and locate shells in injured soldiers. She and Irene traveled with one of the portable X-ray vehicles, trained nurses and radiographers, and convinced the wealthy to donate vehicles for the cause. Over a million soldiers were treated due to Marie's innovations.

Radioactive fall-out. There was a terrible downside to working for years with radioactive elements and there is no doubt that Madame Curie was exposed to high levels of radiation. Her husband was reportedly already suffering from bone cancer when he died. In a paper written in 1901, her husband described the effects of skin exposure to radium: "The skin became red . . . it looked like a burn, but was scarcely painful. After several days the red area without enlarging grew redder; on the twentieth day scabs formed and when they fell away they left a deep wound. . . . We have suffered from various changes in our hands during researches. The skin of the hands scales; the tips of the fingers . . . become hard and sometimes extremely painful; one of us had inflamed fingertips for a fortnight, which subsided with scaling but at the end of two months were still painful."[4] These superficial symptoms were minor compared to the damage that was being done under the skin by the accumulation and release of radioactivity.

In addition to fatigue, weight loss, anemia, and severe headaches, radiation sickness can result in cognitive dysfunction, mental dullness, and memory loss. As you may have noticed, several of the symptoms of radiation sickness are identical to the symptoms of depression. In fact, it is likely that Marie's increasing struggle with depression throughout her life intensified with the accumulation of radioactive elements in her system. In 1934, Marie Curie died of aplastic pernicious anemia, now known as leukemia. Her disease was caused by exposure to the elements that she worked to understand.

Conclusion

Marie Curie suffered from symptoms of depression and experienced extremely stressful life events including the deaths of loved ones and scrutiny from the paparazzi. However, her drive to learn more about her area of science continuously drove her back to her laboratory and helped her be resilient in the face of challenges. She fought for her right to attain advanced education and pursue research in radioactivity and it led her to two Nobel Prizes and death. Now that's commitment.

4. Becquerel, H. & Curie, P. (1901). "Action Physiologiques des rayons du radium," paper given at the French Academy of Science.

Diagnosis

Axis I: Major depressive episode, Moderate severity; Bereavement; Occupational problems

Axis II: No diagnosis

Axis III: Radiation poisoning; Leukemia

Axis IV: Lived with intense media scrutiny

Axis V: GAF = 70–mild symptoms: transient depression; impairment to social functioning

DR. HENRY JEKYLL

(AND MR. EDWARD HYDE)

(First appeared in Robert Louis Stevenson's novel *Dr. Jekyll and Mr. Hyde*, 1931)

*"Oh, God. I've gone further than man should go.
Forgive me. Help me!"*
—Dr. Jekyll

Nationality: English
Primary goals: Have his cake and eat it, too
Hair: Sometimes well coiffed, other times matted
Likes: Pushing down children
Dislikes: Nosy lawyers
Origin: The nightmares of author Robert Louis Stevenson

Genius:

Madness:

Introduction

The good doctor was popularized in a novella titled *The Strange Case of Dr. Jekyll and Mr. Hyde* written by Robert Louis Stevenson in 1886, but some may be more familiar with him as satirized in old episodes of Looney Toons.[1] His story is simple: after a bout of notorious self-experimentation, Dr. Henry Jekyll was stripped of his M.D. and personally introduced to the terrifying Mr. Edward Hyde.

Portrait of a Scientist

No explicit evidence of Dr. Jekyll's childhood exists, but we can infer that he was raised in a relatively high-class family. Not only was he able to attend medical school, but he keeps company with members of high society, including lawyers and scientists. Additionally, Stevenson describes Dr. Jekyll's home as having "a great air of wealth and comfort." Despite (or because of) his high social standing, it is this struggle between his own inner demons and the expectations of society that sets the stage for Dr. Jekyll's horrible ordeal.

This inner struggle is fertile soil for *psychoanalysts*—therapists who ascribe to the psychoanalytic theories that originated with Sigmund Freud. A number of psychoanalytic hypotheses might arise about what events and circumstances in Dr. Jekyll's childhood might have led to his bizarre adult behaviors. For example, Freud's original tripartite model of the human psyche claims that the *id*

---

1. In a number of 1950s Looney Tunes cartoons, Tweety Bird has access to a special formula that is similar to Dr. Jekyll's. Upon ingestion, Tweety is transformed into a giant bird with super strength, capable of eating Sylvester the cat.

produces animal impulses and the *super-ego* constantly tries to suppress these impulses with conscience, while the *ego* is the negotiator who must satisfy the id in acceptable ways that placate the super-ego. In short, the human id is motivated by raw desire without regard for consequences (what Freud called the pleasure principle), but the ego is governed by the reality principle and charged with helping us achieve pleasure in the context of reality.

A psychoanalyst might hypothesize that events in Dr. Jekyll's childhood caused his personality to become overcontrolled. During a strict and competitve upbringing, Henry Jekyll's straitlaced super-ego became so strong that he felt extraordinarily guilty about his natural pleasure-seeking impulses and was compelled to create an alter-ego under which he could let out his true underlying base impulses. Under great social pressure, the super-ego and id were forced apart and manifested as two different individuals inhabiting the same body—one chaste and one murderously evil.

Although this split occurred when Dr. Jekyll was an adult, under Freud's model the problem was brewing long before. According to Freud, character and personality traits arise from unconscious conflicts during childhood development. When unconscious needs for sex and aggression are over- or underindulged during the stages of psychosexual development, neurotic traits can emerge in adulthood. There are a number of developmental stages during which things may have started to go tragically wrong for Dr. Jekyll. Overly strong super-egos can develop when parents are too punitive during the anal stage of development. Strict toilet training may have led young Henry to be "anal" and overcontrolled as an adult. Overly strict parenting during the latency phase may have also contributed to a sense of self-shame, as Freud believed that the super-ego develops when messages about right and wrong are internalized from our parents. Had the adult Dr. Jekyll taken the time to walk into a psychoanalyst's office, he might have been able to explore some of his childhood issues and hence avert the tragic development of his killer alter-ego—Edward Hyde.

Scientific Accomplishments

In modern-day terms, Dr. Jekyll would probably best be termed a biomedical engineer, or perhaps a molecular biologist. In his training as a medical doctor, Dr. Jekyll learned the inner workings of a properly functioning human body, as well as the gross physical pathologies of disease processes. It is worth noting that Dr. Jekyll devoted significant time to charity medical work, providing medical assistance to the poor underclass. At the time, the poor of England were likely to have a number of vile but common diseases, such as gout, cholera, influenza, fevers, tuberculosis, and smallpox. Treatment for these diseases was rudimentary and often included isolation and "advanced" techniques such as bleeding and purging treatments, or recommending that patients drink the milk and blood of cows who grazed exclusively in churchyards. Given the infantile state of medicine at the time, it's a true testament to Dr. Jekyll's intellectual abilities that he was capable of developing the transformative potion that became his undoing.

Dr. Jekyll's initial purpose in developing the potion is to separate man's evil nature from his good nature, to allow his good nature to be more pure and to eliminate the inner battle between good and evil that every man experiences. The potion worked perfectly, completely isolating the evil aspects of Jekyll's personality into the distinct persona of the lustful and evil Edward Hyde. This transformation was also physical; Hyde was smaller, hunched, shriveled, and had hairy, clawlike hands. After taking the formula a few times, Dr. Jekyll begins to enjoy the vile things that he indulges in when under control of his evil nature, presumably while not staining his own "immortal soul." Sadly, problems arose. Although Dr. Jeykll thoughtfully developed an antidote to transform himself back into his normal state, over time he discovered that the frequency of the dosage increased to keep himself from transforming back into Hyde. Inevitably, Jekyll simply ran out of ingredients.

Despite the relatively poor outcomes associated with his experiments, Dr. Jekyll's biochemical accomplishments are remarkable. To date, no other scientists have been able to develop a formula that results in both physical and moral transformation, and is reversible.[2] Unfortunately for us, all that Dr. Henry Jekyll left behind was a confession. The ingredients of his formulas are lost forever.[3]

Edward Hyde's Criminality

Mr. Hyde's reputation for being evil, vile, base, and terrible is justified given his criminal behaviors. On his best behavior, Mr. Hyde intentionally tramples a young girl in the street, terrifying her with his misshapen face and hairy hands. At his worst, he brutally murders a member of parliament by beating him with a cane. Edward is also unrepentantly involved in astonishing a fellow doctor to death upon his watching Edward transform into his dear friend Henry. It can be argued that Hyde ultimately finds redemption, however. After indulging his evil nature at the cost of friends, colleagues, and his alter-ego, Edward Hyde decides to kill himself,

2. Notably, the CIA chemist Dr. Sidney Gottlieb tried unsuccessfully to synthesize hallucinogens that could separate the uncommunicative superego of captured spies to a much more pliable, ego-driven segment of the personality.

3. Dr. Calvin Zabo, a Marvel comics supervillain, is convinced that Dr. Jekyll's secret formula is possible to recreate. He experiments with hormones and succeeds in transforming himself into a very large and dangerous "Mister Hyde."

taking the formerly good Dr. Jekyll with him. Aside from directly and indirectly causing death, Dr. Jekyll's final confession also refers to other criminal and sociopathic behaviors that Mr. Hyde engages in during his exploits. These "forbidden pleasures" are only vaguely described, but likely included sexual interactions with prostitutes, petty thievery, and skulking around menacingly in disreputable back alleys.

Psychopathology: Who's Crazy Here?

In popular culture, the term *schizophrenia* or *schizo* is often used incorrectly to refer to a diagnosis of multiple personality disorder. The root of the term, *schizo,* literally means split, but in a technical sense schizophrenia means split from reality, not a split personality. Individuals with schizophrenia are split from reality in the sense that they exhibit positive symptoms of a disconnect from reality, such as hallucinations, delusions, disorganized speech, or disorganized behavior. Schizophrenia is also characterized by negative symptoms, which include flat affect or emotions, lack of speech, or lack of action. Individuals with schizophrenia who are not treated can be observed talking or yelling to themselves and have trouble navigating everyday tasks. In contrast, both Dr. Jekyll and Mr. Hyde are aware of and connected to reality (the doctor manages to throw dinner parties and Mr. Hyde succeeds in hiring prostitutes), so neither personality meets the diagnostic criteria for schizophrenia.

Although he is not suffering from schizophrenia, there is no doubt that Dr. Jekyll exhibits symptoms of *multiple personality disorder,* a controversial diagnosis that in modern diagnostic terms is known as *dissociative identity disorder*. Major personal trauma is thought to be the *etiology,* or source of this disorder. Individuals with dissociative identity disorder have two or more distinct personality states, each of which has its own perceptions of the world.

Additionally, two or more of these identities must recurrently take control of the individual. Dr. Jekyll definitely exhibits these symptoms. However, he fails to meet the full diagnostic criteria because he has no trouble recalling what he did as Mr. Hyde (individuals with the disorder are unable to recall important information and events experienced by alter-egos). Additionally, to be diagnosed with dissociative identity disorder, the dissociative symptoms must *not* be due to the effects of a substance. In the beginning at least, Dr. Jekyll must consume a secret chemical formula before he is taken over by Mr. Hyde.

Substance Use and Addiction

Dr. Jekyll was transformed into Mr. Hyde by consumption of a special chemical formula that not only made him hunched, ugly, and vile, but also caused him to lose all inhibitions and behave like a sociopath. What was this substance: marijuana? PCP? goof balls? We'll never know exactly, and modern science has not developed anything similar—it would take a remarkable feat of genetic engineering to cause the sort of repeated physical transformations experienced by Dr. Jekyll. However, there are a number of commonly ingested substances that lead to lack of inhibition and it is fair to argue that Dr. Jekyll's *expectations* about what he was taking may have accounted for some of the changes in his behavior.

In the 1970s and 1980s, psychologists at the University of Washington studying addictive behaviors developed a novel approach for studying people's expectations about substance use, particularly alcohol. Their methods depended on the *placebo effect,* in which a *placebo,* a chemically inert or neutral substance, actually changes a person's behavior or illness symptoms based solely on their expectations. In the middle of a psychology building, these enterprising researchers built a realistic (and somewhat seedy) bar. A number of experiments were conducted in which groups of college students were blindfolded and brought to the "bar lab." Subjects were told that they were drinking alcoholic or non-alcoholic beverages and were then either given real alcoholic beverages or non-alcoholic beverages that smelled and tasted alcoholic.[4] The drunkenness that ensued was amusing (and video-recorded), and most remarkably, people who did not ingest alcohol routinely behaved like sloppy, drunken fools. In fact, the placebo drinkers were just as likely as actual drinkers to flirt with the other subjects, have trouble keeping their balance, and dance on the tables. When subjects expected to get uninhibited, they darn well got uninhibited. In later studies, researchers found that when subjects expected alcohol would make them more aggressive, it made them more aggressive.

Thus, whatever strange chemicals Dr. Jekyll was taking, the impact they had on his behavior may have been due to these *expectancy effects,* in which people commonly use substance use as a convenient excuse for bad behavior. Jekyll may have expected that the formula would lead to "uncontrollable" impulses, when in fact the formula simply provided him with an excuse to engage in his id impulses.

There is also substantial evidence that Dr. Jekyll was addicted to his own formula. In his confession, he writes that he tried to keep himself from taking the potion, but was unable to control his desire for taking it, even after seeing the horrible effects of the potion. Dr. Jekyll was able to keep himself from taking the potion for two months, but then relapsed. This phenomenon of experiencing cravings for a substance and being unable to keep oneself from acting on the craving is a common symptom of *substance dependence.* Indi-

---

4. Extreme precautions were taken to ensure that the non-alcohol tasted and smelled exactly like the real alcohol, including several "pleasant evenings" in which experimenters sampled assorted formulas and concentrations.

viduals who are dependent on substances often try to stop using the substance, yet continue despite understanding the problems caused by substance use.

Conclusion

Dr. Jekyll's battle with his alter-ego Mr. Hyde could have arisen from a strict childhood upbringing, the effect of a toxic chemical substance, or simply from his own expectations about what would happen when he took his secret formula. Regardless, Dr. Jekyll's madness led him to take his self-experimentation and quest for knowledge too far. In the end, Dr. Jekyll's unmonitored home science experiments resulted in murderous rampages, the loss of relationships, and self-destruction.

Diagnosis

Axis I: Dissociative identity disorder; Substance-induced manic episodes, Severe, Recurrent; Other substance abuse (substance unknown)

Axis II: No diagnosis

Axis III: No diagnosis

Axis IV: No diagnosis

Axis V: GAF = 25–very serious impairment: suicidal preoccupation; recurring substance abuse

JACK WHITESIDE PARSONS

(1914–1952)

"Freedom is a two-edged sword."
—Jack Parsons

Primary goals: Rocketry
Given name: Marvel[1]
Religion: Worshipping Aleister Crowley
Arch-nemesis: L. Ron Hubbard
Hobby: Sex orgies; summoning demons
FBI file length: 200 pages
Lesser known invention: Parson's Poison Punch, a potent alcoholic concoction

1. Jack was named after his father (whose first name was Marvel), but after a bitter divorce his mother renamed him John Whiteside Parsons.

Genius:

Madness:

Introduction

Known as the "father of space travel," Jack Parsons was not only a brilliant rocket scientist, but an acclaimed occultist. He was a researcher at the California Institute of Technology and a founder of the Jet Propulsion Laboratory in Pasadena. Parsons struggled in his personal relationships and seemed to always be seeking the approval of others. A childish open-mindedness pervaded everything from his ideas about space travel to his belief in the occult, making Jack Parsons the only mad scientist who was also an enigmatic cult leader. A self-proclaimed "anti-Christ," Parsons was set to conquer the planet until L. Ron Hubbard stole his fortune and his girlfriend.

Portrait of a Scientist

Jack Whiteside Parsons did not have an average Pasadena childhood. He was raised on his grandfather's sprawling estate in Pasadena, California, while nearby Los Angeles was exploding in population, buoyed by the booming movie industry. His grandfather, Walter Whiteside, had a number of servants and had made his fortune manufacturing farm equipment and automobiles in the Midwest. Even as a child, Jack was no stranger to wealth and glamour. The young master was educated by tutors and governesses until about age twelve. His interactions with family were so rare that Jack reportedly developed a British accent from interacting with the household help. It was in this lavish, isolated setting that this future rocket scientist steeped himself in classic literature and science fiction magazines.

In this garden paradise, Jack also built his first rockets. He was enamored with the idea of space travel and rocketry from a very young age and often followed the do-it-yourself instructions on the backs of magazines and serials to piece together homemade model rockets. At the time, fireworks and powerfully explosive ingredients were legal and readily available to young boys with plenty of cash. But Jack was not the only boy in the neighborhood interested in explosives; the then-empty desert just outside Pasadena was known as a place where kids would get together after school and on weekends to play with fire. Jack's permissive (some might say dismissive) upbringing allowed him the freedom and free-flowing cash necessary to explore the basics of rocketry in his own nearby desert backyard.

Dyslexia, Peer Rejection, and Friendship

Unfortunately for Jack, his sheltered background did not make him very popular once he transitioned to a public junior high school. Moving into school after being home-schooled can be a stressful transition for any child, but Jack faced additional challenges. Dropped off to school by a limousine and forced to wear a suit and tie, Jack grew his hair long and buried his nose in science fiction magazines. The other kids teased Jack mercilessly, calling him a "girl" or a "mommy's boy," and pulling his long hair. Unpopular with his male peers, Jack chose to retreat into the safety of science fiction.

Despite being an avid reader, however, Jack reportedly suffered from *dyslexia*—a learning disorder in which a child of normal intelligence is impaired in the area of written language, specifically reading and writing. Children with learning disorders often experience rejection from their peers in early adolescence, as other children begin to notice the difficulties they have completing school work or participating in classroom activities. In Jack's case, his learning disorder may have contributed even further to the peer rejection he endured due to socioeconomic differences.

Peer rejection of this magnitude is no laughing matter. In one extreme instance, Jack was beaten severely on the playground. It may be amusing to picture a dapper young rich kid having his crisply ironed shirts sullied in a playground scuffle, but the reality of violence at school is sobering. In fact, research has shown that children who experience peer rejection are more likely to suffer from depression as adults. Negative school experiences can also keep children from forming social connections and engaging fully in their studies.

Fortunately for Jack, he had one friend—Ed Forman. Both Ed and Jack were intelligent boys who did well in school despite having learning disorders. The difference was that Ed was good looking and popular, with much more social capital than Jack. Nevertheless, the boys bonded over a love of rockets and adventure. Like Auguste Piccard, both boys were sensation seekers and loved the thrill of hearing a rocket launch and seeing it disappear into the sky. Ed's father was an engineer, which (with some help from Walter Whiteside's bank account) gave the boys access to tools and expertise to pour into building bigger and better rockets. When Jack's mother sent him to a private boarding school during high school, Jack blew up the toilets and got sent back to regular high school, cementing his reputation as a reckless powder monkey. By the time they entered high school in 1929, the two boys had made a serious commitment to rocketry—their motto, *ad astra per aspera,* meant "through rough ways to the stars." Jack Parsons never completed a formal college education.

Psychopathology: Fascination with the Occult or Dependent Personality Disorder?

Jack's fascination with the occult also began before high school. He reportedly tried to summon the devil into his bedroom around age twelve. Later in life, he claimed that he had succeeded. By the time he was in his early twenties Jack and his first wife, Helen, began attending the Gnostic Mass of the Church of Thelema. Church founder Aleister Crowley—a British magician—preached a hedonistic message that people should do what they want, seeking nothing but their own pleasure. Crowley also claimed that a spiritual entity had entered him to help him write the bible that the church followed. Church members routinely performed rituals to summon ancient spirits and altered their consciousness so they could speak with beings on the spirit plane. The ceremonies were blatantly sexual, and they usually called on numerous cosmological beings that had been made up by Crowley. By the end of the black mass, attendees were usually taking sexual pleasures with each other. Jack was strangely drawn to the leader of the local church, Wilfred Smith, and wanted to learn more about him and the mystical teachings he offered.

Jack was open-minded enough to believe in new cosmological gods and to have faith in the human ability to summon spirits, so it comes as no surprise that he was radically open-minded about other things as well. In the 1930s, he attended meetings about communism that led to questioning by the FBI later in his life. He and his rocketeer friends openly discussed Marxism, erotic poetry, and other risqué topics. Jack's receptive personality led him to develop a sincere belief in the church's teachings about sexual freedom, which said that monogamy was a joke and out of line with people's true will—which was to have sexual relations with whomever they pleased. As such, he started having an affair with his wife Helen's seventeen-year-old stepsister, Betty. This was upsetting for Helen,[2] and she sought comfort with the elderly Wilfred Smith, ultimately living with him. A flexible viewpoint seemingly carried Jack through this situation, as all four of them later lived together in a sprawling new home, the Agape Lodge, that Jack purchased for the growing Los Angeles Church of Thelema. After Crowley became displeased with Smith's leadership and removed him from power, Jack and L. Ron Hubbard stepped into the role of leading the congregation.

As a child Jack had few friends and as an adult Jack was eager to please all of his friends, even those who took advantage of him. While wanting to please others is not always pathological, when taken to extremes it can be very problematic and is a symptom of *dependent personality disorder*. Individuals with this disorder often have difficulty expressing disagreement with others because of fear of loss of approval; they may go to excessive lengths to obtain support from others, often volunteering to do unpleasant things. Jack shows a number of similar behaviors. He was reportedly too much of a good host, once allowing a friend who said he would stay for a couple of days to stay for weeks as he could not manage to tell the friend to leave. He allowed L. Ron Hubbard to develop a close sexual relationship with his wife Helen and even purchased the church a larger home so they could all live together and house other members as well. Eventually Jack divorced Helen and married the younger Betty. In another effort to please Smith and Hubbard, Jack gave all of his salary to the church for the running of the house.

2. Helen was not upset by Jack having an affair, but was upset because the affair was with her stepsister.

Jack's lack of a relationship with his own father may have con-tributed to this desire to please others, particularly the men he saw as father figures. In a letter to Wilfred Smith, he refers to Smith as the father he never had. These dependency symptoms may also have been due to ego-weakness and emotional vulnerability, which research has shown are some of the problems associated with recruitment into cults or new religious movements.

Risk Taking and Rule Breaking: Now That's Rocket Science

Jack Parsons was very intelligent but rarely followed the strict rules of science. This may be because he did not follow the traditional educational path to rocket research. Instead, Jack took a job with the Halifax Powder Company at age twenty, in a relatively low-level position. The money from this job funded the Rocket Research Group, which was basically a rocket gang comprising Jack and his friends. After serving as an expert witness in a trial involv-ing an explosive, Jack was largely accepted as a rocket expert. He was hired to work at the fledgling Jet Propulsion Laboratory at the California Institute of Technology and quickly became the leader of the "Suicide Squad," a group of experimenters committed to learn-ing everything they could about rocket design and the explosive fuels that powered them. Jack was tenacious and methodical about experimenting with different shapes and combinations of powders, and even set up a personal laboratory in his own home. In 1936 Jack helped establish AeroJet, a private company that provided fuels and jet engines to airline companies and the military.

In the 1920s and 1930s, rocket science was not considered a "real" science. Instead, it was closely linked to science fiction; rocket scientists were considered to be zany hobbyists. But Jack Parsons was destined to bring rocketry out of the fringe and into the realm of the attainable. Jack's most important moment of inspiration came when he developed an entirely new class of rocket fuels known as *castable* fuels. These substances were solid fuels, but no longer in the form of powder or pellets. Instead, they began as liquids and then hardened, much like tar or asphalt. Jack's work on the development of these fuels set the stage for feasible space travel with plasticized explosives.

Tragic Endings

Jack's involvement in rocketry ended badly. In the late 1940s he was working for Hughes Aircraft and was accused of treason after he smuggled top-secret documents out of the office to share with the Israeli government, where he was applying for a job leading their rocket program. This job fell through and Jack ended up working on special effects for movies instead.

Jack's involvement in the occult also ended badly. He had aims of leading the Church of Thelema and hoped to eventually take over Crowley's mantle. Unfortunately for Parsons, L. Ron Hubbard was more crafty and eventually led Thelema's followers to the new religion of Scientology. Worse yet, L. Ron Hubbard reportedly took advantage of Parson's belief in the occult and is rumored to have turned the power off and on when Jack was doing his rituals, in order to reinforce Jack's beliefs. The men were close friends, but L. Ron Hubbard also seduced Betty, Jack's young new wife, and convinced Jack to give them all of his money. Hubbard whisked Betty off for a months-long romantic vacation on a yacht, a trip that Parson's cash had funded.[3]

But the unfortunate ending of Jack's second marriage pales in

3. In addition to hanging out with the founder of Scientology, Jack spent time with other famous science fiction authors, such as Isaac Asimov and Robert Heinlein.

comparison to his final ending. In 1952, Parsons accidentally blew himself up and obliterated much of his house in a chemical explosion. He was rushing to complete an order for an explosive special effect before leaving on a long trip to Mexico, and was using a tin can to mix explosive ingredients. Parsons had recently been forced to move his vast collection of highly explosive and unusual chemicals out of a warehouse and into his own home. Unfortunately, Parsons was working that day in his basement surrounded by large quantities of nitroglycerine stored haphazardly in cardboard boxes. Parsons had risked personal injury and death working with dangerous chemicals and explosives for his entire life, but on this day either his luck ran out by accident or Jack took his own life, realizing that the Church of Thelema was a fraud. Either way, Jack Parsons died in the name of science. In response to Jack's death, his mother took her own life, adding even more tragedy to Parsons' ending.

Conclusion

It is likely that due to a cold childhood, Jack Parsons grew up seeking the approval of older men—even to the point of his own ruin. Despite being a tenacious scientist with a brilliant intuition for rocketry, Parsons was repeatedly taken advantage of throughout his life. Even so, Parsons converted the science fiction idea of rocket-powered spacecraft, which had existed since the writings of H. G. Wells, into scientific fact. Jack's success and failures can both be attributed to his open-mindedness. Though his willingness to believe got Jack into trouble in his relationships and almost brought him to economic ruin, without his almost childlike gullibility it is arguable whether Jack Parsons would ever have carried humankind into the age of rockets.

Diagnosis

Axis I: Academic problems; Learning disorder of written expression (previously dyslexia)

Axis II: Dependent personality disorder

Axis III: No diagnosis

Axis IV: Unusual living situation (in an occult religion–shared house)

Axis V: GAF = 75–slight impairment: transient social problems arising from novel living situation; dangerous job

Not Mad, Just Angry

Eccentric scientists don't have time to deal with regular people like you and me. Focused on last-ditch efforts to save the planet or doomsday weapons to destroy it, they can't be bothered with the details of daily life. Yet even the most distracted scientists depend on regular businessmen and politicians for the money necessary to fuel their inventive drives. But business smarts aren't always on par with scientific ability, which can lead very smart people to make very dumb decisions.

This section focuses on a group of scientists whose genius is only rivaled by their sustained rage at other scientists, big corporations, and of course, young people. As geniuses race toward scientific goals, sometimes they can stumble and trip over the mundane particulars of business and work—and this can make them very, very angry.

OLIVER HEAVISIDE

(1850–1925)

"It is wonderful what the brain will stand; break and mend again. I have often wondered that I am not in a madhouse, incurably imbecile, brains all smashed and mixed up."
—Oliver Heaviside

Nationality: English
Primary goals: Revolutionize all of science; keep neighbor kids off the lawn
Hair: Red, parted in the middle, flat on top
Eyes: Piercing, reported to frighten children
Likes: Playing the Aeolian harp; riding his bicycle
Dislikes: Children
Invented: Coaxial cable, which he patented in 1880
Honors: Fellow of the Royal Society; two craters named in his honor (one on the moon and one on Mars); Faraday medalist

of the Institution of Electrical Engineers; Foreign Honorary
Member of the American Institute of Electrical Engineers

Genius:

Madness:

Introduction

In his prime, Dr. Heaviside was a real-life mathematical juggernaut
who never played by the rules. Although he was a pioneer in the
theory of electromagnetism, Heaviside never took a real job as a
professor or an engineer. Instead, he worked math problems at
home and spent most of his life mooching off his parents and siblings. As an older, established mathematician, Heaviside became a
freelance math mercenary—solving equations for cash. Even with
the respect of the mathematics community, a decent pension from
the English government, and a slew of prestigious awards, Heaviside could never stand being around other people (or vice versa).
After an amazingly prolific career, Heaviside ended up as a hermit
with serious psychopathological problems living in a remote sea-
side town. Witnesses say that in his later years, Heaviside could
usually be found in his garden, muttering angrily and covered in
filth—save for his perfectly manicured, cherry-pink fingernails.

Portrait of a Scientist

Oliver was born in the worst, roughest, most filthy slum that
nineteenth-century London had to offer—Camden Town, the same
neighborhood of a young Charles Dickens. Along with his four
older brothers, Oliver struggled not only to survive in this pol-

luted, dangerous environment, but also to avoid being beaten by their belligerent father. Fortunately, Oliver's mother, a school teacher, educated the boy. Despite having a brilliant mind for mathematics, Oliver stubbornly refused to study other subjects that he saw as pointless.[1]

As a young boy, Oliver contracted scarlet fever, which left him partially deaf. Later in life, he reported that this disability left him unable to play with other children. Recent research indicates that severe childhood illnesses can have a major impact on child development and on family interactions. Children who experience extended illness are at increased risk for developmental and cognitive delays. Oliver's deafness most likely did lead to difficulties with his social development, although there is no evidence of cognitive delays.

The odds were against Oliver from the start—until the arrival of Sir Charles Wheatstone. While Oliver was a teenager, his sister managed to marry Sir Wheatstone, who was an incredibly successful electrical engineer for hire. Wheatstone very likely provided a positive *role model* of a prosperous scientist to Oliver and his brothers (who lived in fear of their real father). Although young Heaviside eventually became even more successful than the honorable Sir Wheatstone, his low beginnings seem to have obviated any need for respect from others.[2]

Heaviside was self-educated after age sixteen, which was the last year that he attended school.[3] For two years, he lived at home and

1. In various notes and letters, Heaviside is reported to have written that "the teaching of grammar to children is a barbarous practice, and should be abolished," and that "chemistry is, so far, eminently unmathematical." He also called geometry ". . . a sad farce." (Nahim, P. [2002], 17.)

2. Heaviside's utter lack of care as to whether he is respected is in stark contrast to many other mad scientists who crave respect more than anything (see *Dr. No*, pp. 21–29).

3. Philo Farnsworth was also self-educated, never attending school past his teenage years.

forced himself to study a strict, self-chosen regimen of mathematics and engineering. Afterward, Oliver became a telegraph operator and in that position continued teaching himself the laws of physics and mathematics. Despite being partially deaf and having no venue for formal schooling, Oliver learned Morse code and began to understand the intricate electrical and magnetic workings that allow signals to travel along thousands of miles of telegraph wire. This knowledge was to serve him well during his life as a bachelor mathematician.

Scientific Accomplishments

Oliver Heaviside's scientific and engineering accomplishments are impressive, especially considering his near total lack of formal education. Heaviside independently worked in the areas of physics, mathematics, and engineering. Predictably, much of his work was prompted by a very practical desire to understand and improve telegraph and telephone systems. Heaviside only worked for six years at the telegraph company and then "retired" at the age of twenty-one to devote himself exclusively to research. For example, one early contribution was the idea of putting coils that would increase capacitance along long-distance telephone and telegraph lines in order to reduce signal distortion. This was implemented in the United States by the early 1900s. Moreover, Oliver made a number of contributions to calculus, and his original work changed the way that differential equations were solved in a number of areas.[4]

Additionally, he wrote a three-volume text regarding radio and electrical engineering, which defined a number of basic terms related to AC circuits, including impedance and induction. In 1880, Heaviside patented a special cable which minimized interference between wires

4. It is reported that a copy of *Heaviside's Operational Calculus* was sent to Albert Einstein, who enthusiastically responded that he was delighted to finally learn Heaviside's "peculiar mathematical witchcraft."

by wrapping an outer wire around an inner one. This new arrangement was the original *coaxial cable*, which is in use everywhere today.

Heaviside also made substantial contributions to theoretical science. In one case, he theorized that the sky had a layer of ionized (i.e., electrically charged) particles. He suggested that this electrical layer reflected radio waves, which could explain how waves are sometimes able to travel all the way around the planet instead of shooting into space. This was proven just before Heaviside's death in 1924. Although a handful of other researchers independently suggested the same thing, Heaviside's description stuck and the layer of atmosphere was initially called the "Heaviside" layer. Today, it is called the ionosphere.

Poor Physical Health

In addition to deafness brought on by childhood illness, Heaviside suffered from a number of major health problems throughout his adult years, some of which became much more serious for him after age forty-five. Although he was an active cyclist and in good health in his middle age, Heaviside's diagnoses included gout and jaundice by the age of forty. He also reportedly suffered from malaria and gallstones.

Gout is a medical condition in which uric acid, a common waste product made by using muscles, is not properly metabolized. Uric acid is overly present in the blood stream and is deposited and crystallizes on the surface of cartilage and tendons in the joints. This can result in pain and swelling, especially of hands, toes, feet, and knee joints. Gout can be exacerbated by alcohol and coffee intake and sometimes leads to kidney stones. *Jaundice* is caused by dysfunction at some point in the liver system, which results in excessive bilirubin in the blood. Symptoms of jaundice include yellowing of the skin and whites of the eyes. Attacks of jaundice are often accompanied by severe fever.

Problems with physical health often lead to reductions in health-related quality of life. *Quality of life* is an individual's perspective on his or her ability to perform everyday tasks and enjoy life. In Heaviside's case, his health-related quality of life was impaired in a number of ways. His ability to do everyday physical tasks was impaired by his gout pain, as he had trouble cleaning and maintaining his home. Oliver's health also impaired his social and professional quality of life, because his pain kept him from corresponding and interacting with colleagues and friends.

Unusual Personality and Physical Features: An Oddity

Oliver Heaviside was described as an eccentric and an odd duck. This was likely due to an amalgamation of unusual features that defined Heaviside. Though these features do not seem to be symptoms of a single psychological disorder, they are certainly atypical and led Heaviside to experience some rejection from other scientists and from his neighbors.

Deafness. Though deafness is largely accepted in society today, it was shunned during Heaviside's time. In fact, it was common for deaf children to be institutionalized because they were assumed to be intellectually inferior. Thus, there were fewer deaf adults living independently. Heaviside was only partially deaf as a child, but these symptoms increased as he aged, making it difficult for him to communicate and causing others to perceive him as being even more odd than he really was.

Unusual sense of humor. Oliver is described as having an "impish" sense of humor and he was reportedly subtle in his sarcasm. This sense of humor was somewhat easily understood in written communication, but was more difficult for others to understand when speaking with Heaviside. In addition, Heaviside often inappropriately included humorous asides in his technical or professional work.

Holds a grudge. By many accounts, Oliver Heaviside had trouble taking criticism and never forgot an insult. He refused an award from a prestigious scientific organization because he was bitter about something a journal editor had written years earlier. When a lifelong rival passed away, Heaviside showed unforgiveness when he wrote on his rival's obituary that he was ". . . an intensely greedy, grasping man." It is also likely that Oliver held grudges against children who made fun of him; he wrote notes about the bad things these children did to him in order to share them with the police, calling them "insolently rude imbeciles."

Never rode in a car. Though automobiles were very common in England by the 1920s, Oliver did not ride in an automobile until his ambulance ride to a hospital in his final days. He preferred to go by bicycle and would ride his bike for great distances despite readily available and much more efficient means of transport.

An unfortunate oddball. Oliver Heaviside was the quintessential odd, reclusive, bachelor neighbor. Unfortunately this made it difficult for others to get to know him and left him socially isolated, particularly in his later years.

Psychopathology: Agoraphobia and Dementia

Evidence suggests that Oliver suffered from symptoms of agoraphobia and dementia, though these symptoms did not emerge until the last few years of his life. *Agoraphobia* is an anxiety disorder in which an individual typically fears being outside of their home, being in a crowd, or traveling in a bus, train, or automobile. Individuals with agoraphobia often experience such high levels of fear and anxiety that they avoid leaving home and are often unable to conquer their fears and return to normal functioning without intervention. In severe cases of agoraphobia, individuals have been known to stay in their homes for decades. Heaviside certainly refused to leave his home later in life and even refused to let others in to assist him at times. He also did not ride in cars, another symptom of agoraphobia.

Heaviside did not seem to be bothered by the fact that he did not leave his house. Instead, the primary symptom that troubled Heaviside was cognitive and memory impairment, the primary symptoms of dementia.[5] He wrote that his illnesses had moved to his brain, which caused him to forget eggs cooking on the stove and to burn things in the oven. Heaviside reportedly signed his letters with the initials "W.O.R.M.," a moniker that meant something only to him. People with symptoms of dementia sometimes have a disturbed or distorted sense of self, including delusions that they are someone else. Heaviside even signed one letter "I am, sir, Yours very truly and anagrammatically, O! He is a very Devil, W.O.R.M.," which was very confusing to the letter's recipient and provides further evidence of Heaviside's cognitive confusion.[6]

Oliver also showed *behavioral disturbances,* which are associated with dementia (and with psychotic disorders). He reportedly began bringing granite blocks inside his home to use as furniture. Heaviside also refused to let friends and neighbors into his home and began what he called a "fight" with Lipton's, a grocery company. Heaviside ranted that the company had sent him sugared milk in

5. See Hubert J. Farnsworth for a more complete description of dementia.

6. Nahim, P. (2002), 238.

tins rather than the pure and unadulterated product that he had ordered and began a lengthy correspondence with the company's headquarters in Sweden. For unknown reasons, he began painting his fingernails with pink polish, perhaps to cover up the yellowing due to jaundice. In sum, Heaviside was a withdrawn man with symptoms of agoraphobia and cognitive and behavioral symptoms of dementia. There are a number of factors that likely contributed to Heaviside's symptoms.

Medical conditions. Heaviside wrote in a letter that his pain and poor health led him to a "violent attack of internal derangement" on at least one occasion. Heaviside's health diagnoses likely contributed to his mental problems.[7] There is substantial evidence that declining physical health, as well as simple digestive system maladies, can lead to increases in dementia symptoms in the elderly. It is also likely that a fall from a ladder and the resulting back injury contributed to Heaviside's final decline in physical and mental health.

Social isolation. Heaviside also isolated himself by living in a relatively small town. He enjoyed working in solitude and spent most of his time reading and writing about science. This extreme introversion led to some persecution from local children, who had no idea that Heaviside was an internationally renowned scientist. It has been reported that kids would throw rocks at Heaviside's windows, graffiti insults on the gate to his yard, yell at him, and steal his fruit.[8]

Permanent bachelor status. Prior to age forty-seven when he moved to Newton Abbot, Oliver lived with his parents, with the

7. Nahim, P. (2002), 295.
8. A child who lived next door to the elderly Oliver Heaviside, Beverley Nichols, later wrote that "[Heaviside] seldom dressed, and was usually attired in a kimono of pale pink silk." (Nichols, B. [1972].)

exception of a three-year stretch when he was a telegraph operator in Denmark. Although living with one's parents until middle age might have been more common in Heaviside's time, it was still unusual for a man not to marry. Research indicates that on average, marriage is beneficial to men's health and well-being. In Heaviside's case, he would have probably benefited socially and physically from having a partner to help care for him.

Conclusion

Heaviside was an unusual character who suffered from serious health problems throughout most of his life. He also experienced clinically significant symptoms of agoraphobia and dementia, as well as serious medical conditions. Despite these challenges and despite a lack of formal education, Heaviside made substantial contributions to mathematics and engineering and changed forever the way differential equations were solved. And honestly, where would we be without the coaxial cable that brings television into our homes?

Diagnosis

Axis I: Occupational problems; Age-related cognitive decline; Agoraphobia; Dementia

Axis II: No diagnosis

Axis III: Gout; Jaundice; Hearing loss; History of scarlet fever

Axis IV: Poor living conditions (house in significant disrepair)

Axis V: GAF = 20—very serious impairment: some danger of hurting self; frequent angry outbursts; fails to maintain minimal personal hygiene

PHILO FARNSWORTH

(1906–1971)

"Television is a gift of God, and God will hold those who utilize his divine instrument accountable to him."
—Philo Farnsworth

Home states: Utah, Idaho
Primary goals: Unlimited electricity for all mankind[1]
Patents: Over 130 U.S. patents and at least 100 foreign patents
Likes: Spending time in his laboratory
Dislikes: Corporate giants, patent attorneys
Fictional counterpart: Professor Hubert J. Farnsworth, of television's *Futurama*
Named after him: Farnsworth Peak, a mountain near Salt Lake City, Utah, that is used for radio and TV broadcasting

1. This is remarkably similar to Tesla's goal of providing wireless electricity to the world.

Genius:

Madness:

Introduction

Bow down and worship him, because Philo Farnsworth invented the electronic television. Unfortunately, his science career fell victim to the corporate radio and television broadcasting giant, RCA. The scientist grew up driving horse-drawn wagons in the country and he died having helped push society into a new electronic age. While most kids these days stare slack jawed at the tube, as a fourteen-year-old, Philo Farnsworth was busy conceiving of the idea for television; he sketched the basic design on a blackboard at his high school. By 1927, the science stud was twenty-one years old and the proud owner of an operating television prototype. Even so, you may have never heard of the man. Despite his remarkable contribution to science, Farnsworth didn't fully understand the importance of his invention until two years before his death, when in 1969 he watched the national broadcast of Neil Armstrong walking on the moon. He also wasn't granted the recognition he deserved for his work until posthumously, when his wife worked to get Farnsworth the credit he deserved. Frustration took a heavy toll on his life and in his later years, Farnsworth suffered from a number of psychological problems. Today, the scientist's fictional counterpart, the wrinkled, fist-shaking Professor Hubert J. Farnsworth of *Futurama,* broadcast on Comedy Central—only one of countless channels that are now available on Philo Farnsworth's "electric image projection system."

Portrait of a Scientist

Philo Farnsworth grew up on his family's farms in Utah and Idaho. The Farnsworth family faced economic difficulties, and so Philo and his four siblings did not always have enough to eat. *Malnutrition* in childhood can have a profound negative affect on children's physical and mental development, but it did not seem to have any long-term effects on Philo. When Philo was a child, radio was just beginning to establish itself in an essential role in American life, and the idea of "radio vision" and other things involving electricity captured Philo's imagination. The Farnsworth family had a radio in the 1920s (as did 14 million other American households by 1930). They also had wagons and livestock, and when the family moved from Utah to Idaho when Philo was eleven years old, he was responsible for driving one of the three family wagons more than five hundred miles to the new Farnsworth homestead. In 1919 the Farnsworths moved to a farm with an electric generator, and Philo quickly established himself as the family electricity expert, stepping in to repair and maintain the generator.

Academically, Philo had limited opportunities as a child. He attended small local schools and amazed teachers with his knowledge about science and his drive to learn about electricity. Despite trying economic circumstances and limited resources, Philo's parents were resourceful and ensured that he got as much education and as many opportunities for success as possible. Much of Farnsworth's knowledge and enthusiasm came from *Science and Invention* magazine, which his father made readily accessible. Philo often chose to read this magazine, tinker with farm equipment, and get lost in his ideas about electricity rather than play with his siblings, practice his violin, or complete his farm chores.

Philo was a successful inventor even as a teenager and spent much of his life intimately involved with radios. He listened to news and other programming on the Farnsworth family radio and devised improvements, such as more accurate tuning knobs. He frequently submitted entries to magazine invention contests and won on a number of occasions. His parents encouraged his inventive endeavors—one of his childhood inventions was a thief-proof ignition switch for automobiles,[2] which won Philo $25.00 in a magazine invention contest. In an ominous foreshadowing of things to come, however, Philo's father sent the prize money to a patent attorney to ensure Philo's ideas were not stolen, but never got a reply.

Television Gets Going

In 1920, Philo was plowing the family fields when he had an inspiration: images could be scanned and broadcast row by row, just like the field he was plowing. This insight was the kernel of understanding that led Philo to invent the *electronic* television. At the time, a number of scientists had devised *mechanical* systems for projecting images that involved small mirrors among other things, but Philo's was the first to involve projecting electrons. In 1922, at the age of fifteen, Philo sketched his idea for an electrical system that would project an image on a blackboard for his high school chemistry teacher. Just five years later, this idea was a reality and an image of Farnsworth's new wife was successfully televised in a demonstration in San Francisco.

This relatively speedy success is remarkable, especially considering that Farnsworth completed the task without substantial financial backing or the support of a major corporation or university. He

2. Car keys were invented some years after cars. Early cars had simple switches that ignited the engine, leaving them vulnerable to theft.

did, however, have his mother's support. Philo's father passed away in 1924 and his mother personally guaranteed that Philo would not waste his time in military service. She wrote a letter to her U.S. senator indicating that the family needed Philo's help on the farm as well as financially. This disappointed the U.S. Navy because Philo had ranked second in the nation on a U.S. Naval Academy aptitude test and had been accepted to the Naval Academy in Annapolis, Maryland. Philo attended some college at Brigham Young University, working odd jobs to put himself through school, but felt he and his family could not afford it.

By 1926, Philo was known as Phil. Phil finally got serious about his television research and opened a radio sales and repair shop with his brother-in-law in Salt Lake City. This allowed him to spend all his free time working on television and obtain initial funding to set up research. After marrying his wife, Elma, Phil obtained investor funding and moved his radio shop and laboratory to San Francisco, where their apartment housed the first television experiments.

Technology: What Comes After You Invent Television?

Farnsworth's work as an inventor and scientist did not stop after television. In the 1930s, his work perfected the technologies needed to bring brighter and more precise television images. He also created several portable television cameras, which he demonstrated by filming popular sports like the Philadelphia Eagles playing football and live entertainment such as tap dancing. One of his cameras was used to film the 1936 Olympic Games. Phil continued actively inventing during World War II and his companies increasingly received support from the military. Working from a lab in Maine, Farnsworth provided high-level direction for his corporate research. The research occurring at this time contributed to the guided bomb—television guided, to be exact. Placed in a bomb, Farnsworth's "image dissector tube" relayed what the bomb "saw" back to headquarters. Eventually, this research led to footage of Neil Armstrong taking the first steps on the moon.

The Farnsworth Empire

In typical mad scientist fashion,[3] Farnsworth had a tendency to name his companies and his creations after himself. Following are companies he was directly involved with:

- ϟ Farnsworth Television Laboratories: 1926–35
- ϟ Farnsworth Television Incorporated: 1935–38
- ϟ Farnsworth Television and Radio Corporation: 1938–49
- ϟ Farnsworth Electronics (wholly owned subsidiary of ITT): 1954–58
- ϟ Farnsworth Research Corporation (wholly owned subsidiary of ITT): 1957–67
- ϟ Philo T. Farnsworth and Associates: 1968–71

Note: Farnsworth also worked for the Philco Radio and Television Corporation, but Philco stood for Philadelphia, not Phil.

Psychopathology: Paranoid Personality Disorder, or Justified Indignation?

When he was caught up in a legal battle with RCA, some people accused Farnsworth of being *paranoid* about the company trying to steal his invention or usurp his patents. In fact, evidence suggests that any distrust or suspiciousness Farnsworth demonstrated about

3. For instance, Lex Luthor.

this was probably justified and was not a symptom of a personality disorder. The primary symptom of paranoid personality disorder is that the individual suspects, *without sufficient basis,* that others are exploiting, harming, or deceiving him or her. Farnsworth had more than sufficient basis to suspect that RCA was exploiting him. In fact, Vladimir Zworykin, an engineer working for RCA, was invited to visit Farnsworth's Television Laboratories in the hopes that RCA might want to develop large-scale production of Farnsworth's system. This visit would prompt a decades-long patent battle between Farnsworth and RCA. Zworykin was treated very kindly and given a complete demonstration and explanation of the systems. Soon after, RCA developed suspiciously similar systems and began a public relations campaign dedicated to touting their own system over Farnsworth's. To add insult to injury, RCA then sued Farnsworth, claiming that he was infringing on a 1923 patent of Zworykin's. Ultimately, Farnsworth won the legal battle, in part due to the testimony of his high school chemistry teacher, but not until after years of constant anxiety. Unfortunately for Farnsworth, RCA easily won the public relations battle during this time and climbed to the top in television and radio production. Thus, it is no surprise that Farnsworth was suspicious of large companies. Later in his life he was critical of the patent system, claiming that it hurt small businesses by costing them money and keeping resources away from further research and development.

Stress, Addictions, and Avoidant Coping

Farnsworth experienced a number of major *stressful life events,* and developed a pattern of coping that was sometimes problematic. Stressful life events are not always negative events; they are simply changes in our lives and can include positive life events such as getting married or having a new baby. Unfortunately, many of the stressful life events in Farnsworth's life were negative. His father died when Phil was still a teenager and in 1932 his second son died at thirteen months of age. In response to both of these stressors, Phil is reported to have lost himself in his work. *Coping strategies* are things that people think or do in order to minimize, tolerate, or endure stressful events. Research shows that *active coping strategies* such as dealing directly with problems, telling yourself positive things, or allowing yourself to experience emotions are generally associated with better emotional adjustment following stressors. On the other hand, *avoidant coping strategies* such as emotional withdrawal, distracting oneself from the problem, or using alcohol to avoid the problem are associated with worse adjustment. Farnsworth reportedly engaged in "workaholic" behaviors and sometimes turned to alcohol, not the best way to handle stressful events.

Although Farnsworth reportedly became depressed at times, for most of his life his mood problems never led to *clinically significant distress* or *functional impairment*, a requirement for receiving a mood disorder diagnosis. In fact, it is more likely that Farnsworth suffered from occasional manic episodes that wore him down physically and mentally. For the majority of his life, these episodes were mild. Mild manic episodes *can* result in an elevated mood and increased productivity, but mania typically drives people beyond happiness and into frazzled mental states during which they become increasingly irritable and cannot slow their activity level. Farnsworth was described as driven, even at a young age. He often forgot to eat when he was working on a project because his nervous energy and excitement overcame him. Phil's use of avoidant coping strategies such as throwing himself into his laboratory work in the face of other problems may have prolonged or worsened these episodes. According to his wife, Farnsworth felt he had to drink at times to calm his nerves. Later in life, he suffered at least one nervous breakdown, a vague term which provides us with little information about specific psychological diagnosis. It is likely that this breakdown was the culmination of a manic episode.

Final Years: Fusion

Toward the end of his life, there is some evidence that Farnsworth suffered from mild delusions, some of which centered around fusion power. Phil never thought that television was his most important invention—he believed his "Project Fusor" work on fusion power was his greatest scientific contribution. Though the value of fusion power may yet be proven as nuclear science advances, Farnsworth was certainly deluded about his small laboratory's ability to solve such a huge scientific problem. His fusion theory was a system for creating inexpensive energy that he thought would revolutionize the entire world.[4] From a small research laboratory in Maine, Farnsworth established his last company in 1968, Philo T. Farnsworth and Associates. The mission statement highlighted the company's goal to create "unique theories which may produce solutions to world problems."

The goals of the Fusor project were admirable; however, it was fairly unreasonable for Farnsworth to think that low-budget experimentation could lead to the production of unlimited energy resources. But, Phil reportedly felt he was moving forward and even took out a second mortgage on his house to finance the venture. By 1969, he had acquired five patents related to fusion energy, including the "Electron Gun in the form of a multi-pactor" and the "Microwave Amplifier utilizing multi-paction to produce periodically bunched electrons." As he faced another major life stressor—his own deteriorating health—Phil responded by coping as usual: he worked even harder. He felt an increased desire and pres-

4. Very similar to Tesla's ideas.

sure to work, knowing his remaining time was limited. He was so insistent on working despite his poor health that he had his family bring him into the laboratory on a stretcher.

Farnsworth's Wife and the Other Woman

When he married, Phil Farnsworth reportedly warned his wife about television, the "other woman" in his life. There is no doubt that Elma "Pem" Farnsworth was indispensable, and in fact, Farnsworth claimed "my wife and I started this TV." Where Phil was awkward and shy, Pem was articulate and charming. In many ways, she carried Farnsworth's first company, doing everything from spot welding and mathematics to secretarial and bookkeeping work. She was the first person on the payroll at Farnsworth's Television Laboratories and worked in all of Farnsworth's companies. She gave birth to their four sons, raised them, and kept the family's house in order. In 1942, Phil was in very poor health and was not taking care of himself properly. Pem threatened to leave him, and only this prompted Phil to seek the medical attention he needed. When Farnsworth died, Pem was convinced that RCA had robbed him of the recognition he deserved and worked to correct this. She succeeded in having him inducted into several invention halls of fame, commemorated on a United States postage stamp, and memorialized in the national statuary in Washington, D.C.

Conclusion

Philo Farnsworth was a visionary who made our modern entertainment world possible. His involvement in the business world caused him significant levels of stress, which he did not always cope with positively. In the same way that he had envisioned the way a television would work as a child, at the end of his life Phil envisioned fusion working to create personal power sources, power entire communities, make space exploration possible, purify saltwater for drinking, and control the weather. Driven by curiosity (and a few manic symptoms) throughout his life, Farnsworth died at the age of sixty-four. Had he lived another decade or two, we might already be living his vision of safe, clean, inexpensive power for all mankind.

Diagnosis

Axis I: Occupational problems; Manic or hypomanic episodes, Mild severity
Axis II: No diagnosis
Axis III: No diagnosis
Axis IV: Stressful lawsuit
Axis V: GAF = 70–mild symptoms: occasional manic episodes; meaningful interpersonal relationships

HUBERT J. FARNSWORTH

(First appeared in the animated television
show *Futurama*, 1999)

*"They say madness runs in our family. Some even call
me mad. And why? Because I dare to dream of my
own race of atomic monsters?"*
—Hubert J. Farnsworth, in *Futurama*: "A Fishful of Dollars"

Nationality: Earthican
Primary goals: Create a race of superatomic mutants; take a
nap
Hair: Stylishly bald
Preferred clothing: White lab coats; turtleneck sweaters;
nudity
Likes: Stewed carrots; wearing pajamas; being feared
Dislikes: Ogden Wernstrom
Nickname: The Professor
Awards: The Polluting Medal of Pollution

Genius:

Madness:

Introduction

In the cartoon series *Futurama,* Professor Hubert J. Farnsworth plays the senile genius behind many of the mind-blowing inventions that threaten to save (and sometimes destroy) the city of New New York, the planet Earth, and occasionally the universe as we know it. This elderly mad scientist is named after real-world inventor Philo Farnsworth. One scientist invented television and the other is *on* television, but they were both angry old men who believed they were being constantly persecuted by enemies real and imagined.

Despite being one of the oldest human beings on the planet (he stopped counting at 160), the Professor continues to hold a professorship at Mars University, oversees an interplanetary delivery company, and is often called on by politicians (e.g., Richard Nixon's head) to solve scientific problems of global importance. Despite an active work life, Professor Farnsworth suffers physically and mentally from extreme old age and demonstrates signs of dementia and a disturbing lack of empathy for others.

Portrait of a Scientist

Hubert J. Farnsworth was born in the distant future. Before transitioning to a self-professed "mad scientist," Hubert was a "mad graduate student" for many years. During this time, he made the first of many long-standing enemies in the scientific community.

Citing that penmanship counts, Farnsworth delivered an A- grade to an enraged Ogden Wernstrom, who vowed revenge. The two became lifelong rivals.

After graduate school, Farnsworth began work as a roboticist at MomCorp. The overbearing CEO behind the company, a woman named "Mom," used sex and violence to urge the young scientist to operate against his moral compass and create questionable inventions. For example, she pressured him to build fuel-inefficient robot prototypes that guzzled alcohol and belched extreme amounts of pollution into the atmosphere. These robots proliferated and eventually made Mom one of the richest women on the planet, while causing massive global warming. Despite having a torrid love affair with Mom, Farnsworth eventually tired of her insistence that he make immoral choices in robot construction.

In a last-ditch effort to show Mom a positive invention, he developed "Q.T. McWhiskers," a plush, feline robotic toy that meowed, shot rainbows from its eyes, and showered love and affection everywhere it went. After Mom transformed the Q.T. model into an eight-foot-tall killbot with neutron lasers for eyes and the same alarming tendency to meow, Farnsworth decided to leave the company (and his lover) to begin an independent career as his own boss.

Scientific Accomplishments

A passionate scientist, Farnsworth is not only driven to push the frontiers of scientific possibility but also by an empathetic desire to clean up his own messes. He is also repeatedly willing to put himself (and those around him) in danger after his inventions lead to life-threatening situations. When his super-intelligent monkey escapes, Farnsworth bravely chases it into the Martian jungle. When the design of his robots cause global warming, Farnsworth puts himself in the crosshairs of an orbiting space laser while arranging to have Earth pushed slightly out of orbit to cool it down.

Working from his laboratory and home business, Professor Farnsworth has devised a host of amazing inventions, including:

Intergalactic starship. This advanced prototype spacecraft was developed by Farnsworth to traverse across galaxies in hours, using an inconceivably powerful dark-matter engine. The ship comes armed with phasers, torpedoes, and an unbreakable diamond-filament anchor. In addition, the Professor has built in an "angry dome" on top, which provides a safe area for the Professor to vent his many frustrations.

Smell-o-scope. A telescope-like device that allows the viewer to smell distant astronomical bodies. Every heavenly body has its own scent, with Jupiter smelling like strawberries, Saturn like pine needles, and so on.

Atomic monsters. These five mutant super humans are created to represent Earth in a basketball game against the spacefaring Harlem Globetrotters. Each mutant has its own superpower, ranging from super-stretching abilities to a guy with a cannon in his chest. Farnsworth gives the infant mutants liquefied chronotons to age them in time for the game, a move that nearly destroys the space-time continuum.

Hitler-shark. The Professor laments that while most of the public agrees that saving Hitler's brain is a good thing, transplanting it into the body of a great white shark is going too far.

Farnsworth brand killbots. Sold under the brand name "Farnsworth's Killbots," this hulking metallic murder-bot stands over seven feet tall and sports a rotating buzz saw and an enormous smashing hammer for arms. Despite this terrifying appearance, the killbot is programmed to be gentle, preferring a paddleboat ride to actual fighting.

Gravity pump. The inner workings of Farnsworth's gravity pump are mysterious, but the Professor saved the world from dangerous "time skips" with this invention.

Farnsworth has received many honors as a result of his selfless willingness to use science to save the public from threats he has created. Notably, Farnsworth was awarded Earth's highest honor by Richard Nixon's head: The Polluting Medal of Pollution, which spews puffs of toxic smoke onto its wearer. In addition, Farnsworth has received recognition of friends and politicians for saving the universe from vicious time skips brought on by his harvesting of chronotons, using mind-bending logic to retrieve a box containing our universe (that he created) from a parallel dimension, and donating a doomsday weapon to destroy an orbiting ball of trash about to collide with New New York.

Psychopathology: The Quest for Recognition

Farnsworth desperately seeks recognition and attention, which is a primary symptom of *histrionic personality disorder*. This disorder is characterized by excessive attention seeking, a theatrical self-presentation, and the constant use of physical appearance to draw the attention of others. In Farnsworth's case, he demonstrates such attention-seeking symptoms in a number of contexts.

Quest for scientific acclaim. Farnsworth seeks attention within the scientific community, especially in competition with his arch-nemesis, Ogden Wernstrom. Farnsworth competes against Wernstrom to solve global warming and to design the best killbot. In frustration, he even calls Wernstrom a "glass-headed wallaby."

Enjoys being feared. Farnsworth relishes the attention that he gets out of being a threat to others. At Mars University (where he professes) the motto on the school gates reads "Knowledge Brings Fear." At one point, Hubert agrees to give up one of his doomsday devices to save the city he lives in, but only because he realizes that he has several more and that he can part with one and still be feared.

Exhibitionist tendencies. Farnsworth demonstrates very little modesty. When it's too hot due to global warming he wears a cutoff spandex T-shirt and a pair of tiny Speedos swim trunks. During X-mas holidays he is known to go completely nude.

Loves his adoring public. During an international meeting of scientists in Kyoto, Farnsworth walks down the red carpet surrounded by photographers and screaming fans. He blows kisses to the crowd, clearly basking in the knowledge that he is a famous scientist galaxy-wide.

Life on the Edge: No Room for Empathy

Hubert Farnsworth started the Planet Express delivery service in order to fund his outlandish research and to buy materials for out-of-this-world inventions. As a rogue scientist, Farnsworth is not very empathetic toward his employees. This is likely primarily due to his overwhelming motivation to push his work and his company to new frontiers. However, this results in the reckless endangerment of others.

Cavalier with the lives of others. One of the Professor's old delivery service crews reportedly died on the job by being eaten by a space wasp. This was probably due to a lack of safety precautions. When the Professor suspects that his new crew may have also died, Farnsworth recruits a new batch of crew members before even finding out whether the old ones are alive or not. When there are life-threatening problems, Hubert tends to dismiss the safety of others and focus on how to solve the problem at hand. He does not hesitate to send his crew on missions that he knows may be lethal. This includes trips to the "E. Boli planet," to a robot-controlled planet where humans are shot on sight, and a trip to collect honey from Space Bees (the same journey that killed his last crew entirely). He is also willing to lie, telling his crew that mining ice from a speeding asteroid is safe. Indeed, his willingness to risk the lives of his crew is key to the success of his company, which advertises that "Our crew is replaceable, your package isn't."

Tendency to harvest friends' organs. Farnsworth shows a lack of empathy by treating his employees somewhat like biological assets. On one occasion, he tells an employee that a mission will be perfectly safe, but then asks the captain to bring back the employee's blood if things go wrong (they share a blood type). The Professor is also not above profiting monetarily from the death of his crewmembers, as he intends to harvest their organs: Farnsworth encourages one employee to commit suicide so that he can harvest his liver and is seen carrying a Styrofoam cooler that reads "Leela's Organs."

Lies constantly. It is not clear whether Farnsworth lies for monetary gain or to make his crew more likely to go on dangerous missions that will advance his scientific boundaries. While the

Professor's organ harvesting and crew-exploitation behaviors may advance science, they do not seem to be helping his business's bottom line.

Poor Business Decision Making

The Professor may be a shrewd scientist but his business sense is lacking. Farnsworth invented the modern robot as an employee at MomCorp, yet due to poor business decisions, he remains penniless while Mom has made billions. Robots are in use all over the planet, but Farnsworth apparently allowed MomCorp to keep all the profits. This poor business decision was only the beginning of Farnsworth's sub-par economic choices.

The Professor's Planet Express delivery company is often on the verge of bankruptcy. In one case, a four-dollar bank error in favor of the company significantly affected the bottom line for the entire year. Farnsworth hires family members and friends with little regard for how well they will accomplish their jobs. His delivery team is inept, frequently ditching delivery attempts at the first sign of trouble (or if something good comes on television). The bending unit, called Bender, frequently steals and always shirks actual work. Finally, Farnsworth hires a company doctor of an alien species with little expertise diagnosing human beings. Dr. Zoidberg actually mistakes males for females and has no idea which human orifice is for what, making him a serious business liability (despite being a lovable scamp). When his business inefficiencies are pointed out by his own son, Farnsworth ignores the advice. And in one instance when his ownership of Planet Express is questioned, Farnsworth makes a run for an escape pod and bails from his own failed enterprise.

Family Life

Aside from his romance with Mom, there is no evidence that Farnsworth has had any ongoing subsequent romantic relationships (save for a stint as an age-reversed youth). Despite this, Farnsworth is a family man. He takes good care of his twelve-year-old child, who was cloned off a growth on his back that he removed with a fork. A dutiful father, Farnsworth notices quickly when his cloned son begins copying Bender the robot's televised negative behaviors, which include drinking, smoking, and stealing. Noticing that Bender is a poor role model, or someone who purportedly demonstrates positive behaviors for others to emulate, Farnsworth forms the protest group Fathers Against Rude Television (FART) to protest Bender the robot's annoying presence on television. Farnsworth is even willing to resort to violence on the matter, saying that he's a cold-blooded punk when it comes to protecting his son.

Dementia and Senility

The doddering Professor is more than 160 years old and has been declared officially deceased. The result of his extremely advanced age appears in both physical and mental deficiencies, called functional and cognitive decline.

Physical decline. The Professor wears thick glasses, but does not carry a cane or use a hearing aid. It is obvious that the man is nearly blind and deaf, as he sits in the front row of a movie theater and shouts, "down in front!" He also frequently answers questions with a confused "Wha?," clearly demonstrating that he has not heard the question. In one instance, the Professor delivers an entire lecture on "superdupersymmetric string theory" without noticing that no students have attended the class. Besides hearing and vision loss, Farnsworth also suffers from a genetic disease called "wandering bladder." As a result of his physical frailty, the Professor spends much of his time asleep in an easy chair—even when the automated chair is floating in the air and firing weapons.

Cognitive decline. Memory is one of the fundamental *cognitive*, or thinking skills that humans possess. As we age, our memory and other cognitive functions tend to decline. Memory deficits are the most common deficits in *dementia*, a disorder characterized by declines in multiple cognitive abilities. The Professor evidences a number of symptoms of declining memory, including being incapable of counting down from five to one. His memory loss is also evident when he accidentally presents the same invention (a death clock) to the Academy of Inventors two years in a row, having forgotten that he presented it the year before, and lost. In addition, he often completely contradicts himself. For example, on X-mas eve he agrees not to shoot Bender with a shotgun and then immediately fires on the robot when it appears in good faith. Asked if he remembers agreeing not to fire, he shouts angrily, "No!" In addition to memory deficits, the Professor shows other cognitive deficits such as confusion. At one point when the lights go out Farnsworth shouts, "Oh, I'm blind!"

Conclusion

Professor Hubert Farnsworth is an inventor of unparalleled genius. His complex efforts in the laboratory pay off, as his work is easily translated to solve real-world problems just in time to save the city or planet. Despite saving lives on a grand scale, Farnsworth shows a distinct lack of empathy for individuals, which is largely due to his love of being the center of attention and small consideration for how brilliant inventions may impact other humans. However, he enjoys good relationships with close friends and family members, who stick by him despite his failing physical faculties and angry, fist-shaking rants.

Diagnosis

Axis I: Age-related cognitive decline; Age-related functional decline; Dementia

Axis II: Histrionic personality disorder

Axis III: Hearing loss

Axis IV: No diagnosis

Axis V: GAF = 70–mild symptoms: age-related functional decline; hypersomnia; presents an occasional danger to others

Are You a Mad Scientist?

*"Everybody's a mad scientist, and life is their lab.
We're all trying to experiment to find a way to live, to
solve problems, to fend off madness and chaos."*
—David Cronenberg

The mad scientists honored in this hall of fame have a range of psychological disorders and a unifying interest in knowing more about their field of study. To find out if you have what it takes to be a mad scientist, just take this simple quiz. The results will indicate whether you have the requisite traits, beliefs, and behaviors to make it in the world of mad science, and it may help guide your career choices.

Instructions. Circle the number that indicates how true each of the sentences below is, from "not at all true" to "extremely true." There are no right or wrong answers.

	Not at all true	A little true	Somewhat true	Very true	Extremely true
1. I enjoy solving complex mathematical equations.	0	1	2	3	4
2. I don't think a little violence ever hurt anyone.	0	1	2	3	4
3. I am always thirsty for knowledge.	0	1	2	3	4
4. I would not mind spending 7–10 years working to solve a problem.	0	1	2	3	4
5. My knowledge of poisons is extensive.	0	1	2	3	4
6. I hear sounds or voices that are not really there.	0	1	2	3	4
7. I cackle with glee when I'm about to destroy someone.	0	1	2	3	4
8. I feel contempt for others who lack my superior intelligence.	0	1	2	3	4
9. Reading encyclopedias would be a fun way to spend an afternoon.	0	1	2	3	4

	Not at all true	A little true	Somewhat true	Very true	Extremely true
10. If someone does not admire me sufficiently, I feel they must be destroyed.	0	1	2	3	4
11. Others have said that I work too much or spend too much time working.	0	1	2	3	4
12. Friends or family members think my behaviors are odd or strange.	0	1	2	3	4
13. I greatly enjoy solitude.	0	1	2	3	4
14. I have extremely special skills and abilities.	0	1	2	3	4
15. Rocket science just isn't that difficult.	0	1	2	3	4
16. I would enjoy exploring the farthest reaches of outer space.	0	1	2	3	4
17. My work deserves much more recognition.	0	1	2	3	4
18. I often ponder the expansion of the universe and dark matter.	0	1	2	3	4
19. I enjoy fact-checking *Scientific American* magazine.	0	1	2	3	4
20. I mutter or speak aloud when I am alone.	0	1	2	3	4

Scoring the Mad Scientist Quiz

Write your ratings (0–4) for each item in the open box next to the item number. Sum each column to obtain your SQ and MQ scores.

Name: _____

	SQ Items	MQ Items
1.		
2.		
3.		
4.		
5.		
6.		
7.		
8.		
9.		
10.		
11.		
12.		
13.		
14.		
15.		
16.		
17.		
18.		
19.		
20.		
Sums:	SQ =	MQ =

Interpreting Your SQ (Science Quotient) and MQ (Madness Quotient) Scores

Science Quotient Ranges

0–7: Very Low/Abysmal. You are very unlikely to become a mad scientist because your interest in science and studying is extraordinarily low. Individuals who score in this range have a reduced chance of developing the level of interest in science that is required to be a bona fide mad scientist.

8–15: Low/Poor. You have a low probability of reaching high enough levels of science acumen to become a mad scientist. In short, you care little about scientific topics and have minimal desire to learn more about science. This means you may become a mad criminal (if your madness quotient is high), but you'll probably never be a mad scientist.

16–23: Moderate/Good. You have some interest in science and have a good chance of being able to achieve additional scientific knowledge that might contribute to mad science exploits. Practice makes perfect, so spend some more time with your chemistry set and physics books.

24–31: High/Excellent. Many mad scientists have Science Quotient scores in this range. Individuals with high scores have an excellent probability of achieving scientific prowess and creating astounding inventions. You probably enjoy complex mathematics and experimental designs, and may very well have what it takes to make it as a nerdy, nerdy scientist.

32–40: Very High/Extraordinary. Your interest in science is through the roof and your potential for inventing amazing machines and making breakthrough discoveries is phenomenal. If you score in this range, there is a good chance that you are already a scientist. Individuals scoring in the extraordinary range not only understand science but also experience high levels of enjoyment related to science.

Madness Quotient Ranges

0–7: Very Low/Abysmal. You are very unlikely to become a mad scientist because you are reporting virtually no symptoms of mental instability or psychopathology. With a mental health profile this squeaky clean you might be a scientist, but you'll never be a mad scientist.

8–15: Low/Poor. You are reporting low levels of madness symptoms and are unlikely to develop the higher levels of mental instability needed to become a mad scientist. Your mental and emotional characteristics are likely within the normal range, which is not true of most mad scientists.

16–23: Moderate/Good. You are exhibiting some of the psychopathology symptoms that put the "mad" in mad scientist. This means you have a good chance of expanding and perfecting your repertoire of strange and unusual behaviors. You may be able to achieve a higher madness quotient in the future with practice and/or social neglect.

24–31: High/Excellent. Individuals who report high levels of mad scientist psychopathology have an excellent probability of becoming full-fledged mad scientists. You are reporting many symptoms that are similar to those experienced by the mad scientists in this hall of fame. Combine this with a high science quotient, and your lab coat will go from bright white to bloody and dirty in no time.

32–40: Very High/Extraordinary. You are reporting very high levels of symptoms consistent with the types of psychological problems experienced by mad scientists. If your Science Quotient is also high, grab a Bunsen burner and proceed directly to an underground laboratory.

Overall profile interpretation

If you scored in the High or Very High range on both the Science Quotient and the Madness Quotient, you are well qualified to be a mad scientist. If you scored High or Very High on just the Madness Quotient or just the Science Quotient, you may need to work to improve your score (suggestions are described in the next section). If you scored in the Moderate or Low range on both the Science Quotient and Madness Quotients, you might consider a career as a mad scientist's assistant, servant, or hideously deformed lackey.

Tips on improving your Science Quotient

- ⚡ Keep a field notebook on hand and constantly scribble zoological observations about your pets, friends, and coworkers.

- ⚡ Do not hesitate to test-pilot your own inventions, but remember to tether flying machines to the ground for the first flight.

⚡ If you suspect that you just aren't that smart, make friends with a powerful politician—like Stalin.

⚡ Enjoy science by immersing yourself in the heady experience of scientific discovery: Be the captain of your own experimental submarine-ship, the wielder of your own sharp scalpels, and the demigod of your own race of mutant human-animal hybrids.

⚡ When the victims of your experiments are screaming for mercy, don't just listen impassively—use a decibel meter to determine the loudness and pitch of the shrieks and write down your data.

⚡ If you find that other humans are constantly judging the morality of your scientific research, retreat to a moral safe area—like an abandoned volcanic island.

⚡ Remember to leverage your existing doomsday weapons to secure needed money or materials for further research.

⚡ Don't waste time on pointless details: either throw on a motley collection of clothes chosen randomly off the floor, or wear multiple pairs of identical suits.

⚡ Feel free to experiment liberally with strange new chemicals developed in the lab or collected from lonely excursions into uncharted wilderness.

Tips on improving your Madness Quotient

⚡ Spend more time alone (underground or on an island, if possible).

⚡ If being alone hinders your scientific research, be sure to hire helpers who don't speak the same language as each other, have been lobotomized, and/or have grotesque physical deformities.

⚡ Cultivate strange habits and rituals—they're what make you, you!

⚡ Stop caring about other people.

⚡ Create your own language; speak it exclusively.

⚡ Judge people not by their beauty or intelligence, but by blood type and the shapes of their irises.

⚡ Focus your mind and make mental contact with aliens from Venus, spirits from the beyond, or the raw elemental forces of Nature.

⚡ If you have spent your life seeking to exact revenge upon parties that have wronged you, talk about it! The people around you really want to know about that, I bet.

⚡ Whatever it is, don't be afraid to mutter it out loud.

References

Here's how to find out more about mad scientists and psychology in general.

Baer, J. S., Marlatt, G. A., and McMahon, R. (Eds.), (1993). *Addictive behaviors across the lifespan: Prevention, treatment, and policy issues.* Newbury Park, CA: Sage Publications.

Blass, T. (2004). *The man who shocked the world: The life and legacy of Stanley Milgram.* New York: Basic Books.

Cockburn, A., and St. Clair, J. (1998). *Whiteout: The CIA, drugs, and the press.* New York: Verso. [re. Sidney Gottlieb]

Field, A. (1969). *Auguste Piccard: Captain of space, admiral of the abyss.* Boston: Houghton Mifflin Company.

Frauenfelder, M. (2005). *The world's worst: A guide to the most disgusting, hideous, inept, and dangerous people, places, and things on earth.* New York: Chronicle Books. [includes a chapter on Sidney Gottlieb, "the maddest mad scientist"]

Frayling, C. (2005). *Mad, bad and dangerous? The scientist and the cinema.* London: Reaction Books.

Godfrey, D. (2001). *Philo T. Farnsworth: The father of television.* Salt Lake City, UT: University of Utah Press.

Goldsmith, B. (2005). *Obsessive genius: The inner world of Marie Curie.* New York: W. W. Norton.

Hergé. (1979). *The Adventures of Tintin: Volumes 1–5.* New York: Little, Brown & Company.

Hunt, M. (1993). *The story of psychology*. New York: Doubleday.

Milgram, S. (1974). *Obedience to authority*. New York: Harper-Collins.

Nahin, P. (2002). *Oliver Heaviside: The life, work, and times of an electrical genius of the Victorian Age*. Baltimore: Johns Hopkins University Press.

Nichols, B. (1972). *Father figure*. New York: Simon & Schuster.

Passer, M. W., and Smith, R. E. (2007). *Psychology: The science of mind and behavior* (3rd ed.). Boston: McGraw-Hill.

Pendle, G. (2005). *Strange angel: The otherwordly life of rocket scientist Jack Whiteside Parsons*. Orlando, FL: Harcourt.

Piccard, J. (1961). *Seven miles down: The story of the bathyscaph Trieste*. New York: G.P. Putnam's Sons.

Putnam, S., and Stifter, C. (2005). "Behavioral approach-inhibition in toddlers: Prediction from infancy, positive and negative affective components, and correlations with behavior problems." *Child Development, 76,* 212–226.

Rohner, R. P. (1986). *The warmth dimension: Foundations of parental acceptance-rejection theory*. Newbury Park, CA: Sage Publications.

Roll-Hansen, N. (2005). *The Lysenko effect: The politics of science*. Amherst, NY: Humanity Books.

Schatzkin, P. (2004). *The boy who invented television: A story of inspiration, persistence, and quiet passion*. Terre Haute, IN: Tanglewood Books.

Shelley, Mary. (2004). *Frankenstein*. New York: Simon & Schuster.

Siefer, M. (1996). *Wizard: The life and times of Nikola Tesla; Biography of a genius*. Secaucus, NJ: Carol Publishing Group.

Soyfer, V. (1994). *Lysenko and the tragedy of Soviet science*. New Brunswick, NJ: Rutgers University Press.

Stacy, A., Widaman, K., and Marlatt, G. (1990). "Expectancy models of alcohol abuse." *Journal of Personality and Social Psychology, 58,* 918–928.

Stevenson, Robert Louis. (2002). *The strange case of Dr. Jekyll and Mr. Hyde*. New York: W.W. Norton.

Verne, Jules. (2006), *20,000 Leagues Under the Sea*. New York: Sterling. Unabridged Classics.

Wells, H. G. (1968). *The Island of Dr. Moreau*. Cayce, SC: Magnum.

Zuckerman, M. (1984). "Sensation seeking: A comparative approach to a human trait." *Behavioral and Brain Sciences, 7*, 413–471.

Acknowledgments

Special thanks to our agent, Laurie Fox, who championed this joint venture.

Thanks to Brian Long, a mad physicist whose genius spawned the Mad Scientist collaboration.

Thanks to Adam Korn and Danielle Chiotti at Kensington Books. And to our friends, teachers, and colleagues who provided encouragement and training in science and psychopathology: Chris Atkeson, Hamida Bosmajian, Nicole Bush, Lara Embry, Leo Faddis, Corey Fagan, Stuart Greenberg, Melissa Herman, Jonathan Katz, Erica Kovacs, Wanda Kertzman, Kathleen LaVoy, Liliana Lengua, Robert McMahon, Tonya Palermo, Kurt Freeman, Erin Usher, and Lisa Zaidi.

And finally, here's to you, Johnny Five.